Contents

Introduction vii

One
Getting Through 1

Two
The Power of Referrals 29

Three
Following Up 43

Four
Read the Script 49

Five
Polishing Your Voice 55

Six
Perfecting the Art of Listening 61

Seven
How to Qualify a Prospect 75

Eight
Probing 83

Nine
Reconnecting with Prospects 99

Ten
Key Words and Phrases 107

Eleven
The Presentation 111

Twelve
Handling Objections 145

Thirteen
The Art of the Close 175

Fourteen
Dealing with Difficult Customers 201

Fifteen
Hiring the Perfect Telemarketer 213

Summary
What You Learned in This Book 229

Phone Sales

Phone Sales

THE SCIENCE OF MAKING THE SALE

Kerry Johnson, MBA, Ph.D.

Published 2019 by Gildan Media LLC
aka G&D Media
www.GandDmedia.com

FIRST EDITION 2019

Front Cover design by David Rheinhardt of Pyrographx

Interior design by Meghan Day Healey of Story Horse, LLC

Library of Congress Cataloging-in-Publication Data is available upon request

ISBN: 978-1-7225-0179-2

10 9 8 7 6 5 4 3 2 1

Introduction

In my travels as a speaker and consultant, I've found very few people who have even read a book on doing business on the telephone, yet even face-to-face sales demands a very high level of telephone expertise.

The cost of doing business is increasing. It costs much more to do business face-to-face now than ever before. In fact, a recent study done by the Xerox Corporation showed that seeing a prospect face-to-face costs approximately $300. Obviously, this includes preparation time, secretary time, and travel time. Yet the cost of seeing prospects belly button to belly button exclusively is prohibitive.

We can no longer afford to do business in the future as we have in the past. I frequently consult with companies who send their salespeople out to cold-call face-to-face. Often they're effective, yet they rarely are able to see the right person on a walk-in basis. Even on those face-to-face cold-call appointments, proper telephone follow-ups could be much more useful than a handshake.

One Midwestern company, realizing that their costs were going higher and higher and their profits lower and lower, decided to cut their sales force from five salespeople to one. This one salesperson had practiced the art of selling face-to-face for years and years in his job. Suddenly his production goals were multiplied by five. He had no recourse but to use his time much more wisely. He was forced to use different strategies. He talked both to new prospects and existing clients by phone. Only in those instances where he was sure he would be able to get a sale would he take the time to see a prospect face-to-face.

As you might imagine, profits increased by 300 percent. Sales costs were cut by 90 percent. The company experienced a sizable revenue increase, and coincidentally added twenty new salespeople, producing past their sales goals, by using the phone. It's a shame that the company had to learn to train its salespeople with telephone techniques as a last resort.

Years ago, when I started my business, my goal was to see people face-to-face in order to get them to utilize my consulting services. My primary objective was simply to get a prospect on the telephone, commit him to an appointment to see me, and then try to sell him.

My closing rate was approximately 35 to 40 percent on face-to-face appointments, but through the years, I've found that when I talk to prospects by telephone first, I'm able to close not only face-to-face but also on the telephone. I obviously receive more rejection on the telephone than face-to-face, but that's only because the phone allows me to make more calls than I ever could by seeing prospects (particularly because my clients are now located worldwide). I was making more sales in less time and increasing my company profits.

Shelby Carter, senior vice president for the Xerox Corporation, said that salespeople in America have too much windshield time and not enough contact time with prospects: we spend too much time on the road traveling to appointments and too little time eyeball to eyeball, toenail to toenail with our prospects and clients.

We can no longer afford to conduct business simply by sending an email informing our prospect of our intentions to do business. How often have you received a letter or email with a message that could have been more effectively communicated by telephone? Letters are very expensive to write these days. According to the Dartnell Institute, it costs approximately $10 for a staffer to type a simple letter.

It's also obvious today that America is in the midst of a email glut. We are deluged with spam and junk mail enticing us to buy everything from cars to carpeting and curtains. Emails should only be used to confirm the information provided in a telephone conversation.

Until a few years ago, direct-mail solicitors received approximately a 10 percent response rate. Now they can expect one-fourth to one-half of 1 percent response rate. Email spammers are lucky to get one response out of 10,000 mailings. Out of every 200 snail-mail letters you mail, you're lucky to get one response. Misunderstandings occur much more frequently in emails than on the telephone, but the two working together provide for effective business relationships. Proper use of the telephone allowed me to go from being a local speaker and consultant to being a national and worldwide consultant.

Joe Gandolfo was one of the insurance industry's top producers. A heavy telephone user, he also sold nationwide. He used the phone to service existing client needs and prospect for new business to expand his markets. Before traveling, he simply made an appointment with a qualified prospect. Then Joe turned into the expert from afar. Even an insurance agent from the little town of Lakeland, Florida, is an expert to somebody in Iowa.

A recent McGraw-Hill Corporation study found that over 65 percent of personal sales calls were made on the wrong people. In other words, many prospects who were seen face-to-face were not people who could make a decision to buy a product. The proper and effective use of the telephone would help you at least to qualify your prospect to make sure that when you see him face-to-face, he can make a decision.

Because of the low cost, the telephone should be the first resort and the letter your last. After reading this book, you'll be able to get many more sales on the telephone than you ever could with emails, personal letters, or even face-to-face.

A good example of the striking difference between telephone and letter is an international client I had in New Zealand. This individual, Ian Clarke, and I corresponded for approximately one year way back in 1985. At one point, my letters were reaching New Zealand after two months. While some letters got back within fifteen days, I was appalled at how poor the postal service was between the two countries.

One day I decided to make a phone call to New Zealand. It was expensive, but I got more done in fifteen minutes on the phone than I did from six months of writing letters. A phone call is here and now. An email or letter is so impersonal that it can be easily ignored. You undoubtedly have sent letters to which you never received a response. But it's very difficult not to respond to a telephone call, as long as you can get through to the right person.

Some of the things you'll learn in this book are (1) how to get referrals from existing clients and customers and use them to prospect for new business; (2) how to use referrals to your best advantage; and (3) what to say to a referred prospect in the first fifteen seconds.

I'll also tell you how to use a receptionist to help you get to that prospect. If you've been selling for more than a few weeks, you probably realize that one of the responsibilities of an efficient assistant is to serve as a screen to block you. You'll learn how to get through that assistant and get to your prospect. You'll even learn how to get your prospects to call you back if they are unavailable at the time you call.

You'll learn how to avoid telephone tag and how to arouse your prospect's interest in wanting to talk to you. You'll gain information on ways to avoid getting blown off the telephone within the first thirty to sixty seconds, and on ways to use lists in prospecting for new customers. You'll learn how to create a follow-up system that will help you keep on track, and you'll receive clear direction on how to keep your motivation high even while you get rejected.

You'll learn how to use a script. You'll be able to develop your own verbal outline so that you'll be prepared for anything your prospect says. This script will help you avoid being caught off guard. Since your voice is the most important tool over the telephone, you will learn how to develop it.

During this process, you will increase your listening power. You will learn how to use voice recorders to help you analyze your effectiveness. You'll be given tips on how to get your prospect to tune into your high level of sincerity and to feel a sense of urgency about doing business with you. Possibly the one technique that will generate the greatest amount of sales is determining quickly what your prospect really wants.

In chapter 8, you'll be exposed to many valuable facets of probing. You'll learn how to increase your closing rate even as you increase the amount of useful information you receive on how that prospect will buy from you. Through sophisticated probing, you'll discover what your prospect wants. You'll be able to qualify that prospect, making sure that he's actually the right person to talk to. You'll learn how to access and understand your prospect's key words, and, more significantly, how his mind is organized.

You'll recognize your prospect's easily identifiable buying strategy, which in turn you will use to sell him. You'll be given workable steps on how to reach the decision maker, as well as techniques that you will use as a bridge to take you from the approach stage to qualifying your prospect.

You'll learn how to find out what your prospect considers the most important benefits of your product or service and how to withhold those benefits at one point in order to draw your prospect in more closely. You'll be given effective methods for finding out the process your prospect will go through in making a decision.

You'll learn how to ask the right questions, whether they be structured to get more information from your prospect or just to get yes or no. You'll learn how to prepare your prospect for the second call and how to make them more receptive when you talk a second time. You'll also learn how to end the first call while increasing the prospect's enthusiasm for talking with you again.

Have you ever had a prospect seem uninterested while you presented your product? You'll be given directions on how to present your product benefits, keeping high interest. You'll learn how to match the prospect's needs with your product's features and benefits. You'll gain information on how to reconfirm your prospect's needs before you present your ideas as well as on how to avoid the twelve turn-off phrases.

You'll learn how to develop storytelling techniques to help your prospect get a better idea of how your product will help him. You'll learn how to reference-sell your prospect on your products using benefits. The fifteen-second rule in gaining agreement will help you keep your presentation short as you learn about three reasons why people don't buy. You'll discover how to make sure that your prospect sells himself during the process.

Are you good at cashing in on your prospect's objections? In chapter 12, you'll learn how to handle objections on the telephone. You'll study the four steps for finding out what is really behind the objections and how to cash them in, making an even bigger sale. You'll learn the feel-felt-found technique and what objections really mean. You'll develop methods to make sure your prospect is always proven right, never wrong. You'll find out how to deal with unsurmountable objections such as "I'm not interested" or "I don't buy from people on the telephone."

I'll also give you data on how to close on the telephone. We will focus on two basic closing situations: how to close a face-to-face appointment, and how to close a sale solely from the telephone. You'll learn how to handle both of these situations as well as finding out the three most useful telephone closing techniques. You'll learn the recommend close and why saying the word "because" will help rivet your prospect closer to buying your product.

You'll discover how to transfer urgency in order to get your prospect to buy more quickly. You'll discover techniques on how to increase your prospect's trust while closing, and you'll learn how many times you may have to actually ask your prospect to buy before he says yes.

In chapter 14, on dealing with difficult clients, you'll discover how complaining prospects can become your best customers, and you'll be given statistics on the number of customers that could hurt your business and how to turn them around. You'll learn how to dig up new business by keeping in touch with customers who have already done business with you.

You'll also learn how to cross-sell and how to get customers to increase their purchases after they've made an initial buying decision. You'll find out why customers stop doing business with you. As you understand more about how to keep track of your greatest strengths and weaknesses in dealing with customers, you'll become skilled at playing up those strengths and clearing away the weak points.

In the last chapter, you'll learn how to motivate telephone salespeople. You'll learn information on how to pinpoint, interview, and select the right kind of telephone salespeople and how to coach them in improving their skills. Other information will tell you how, and how much, you should pay telephone salespeople.

I recommend that you read this book at least five times over the next three months. Read it all the way through once every two weeks for maximum impact. Plan to apply every technique the day you read about it. If you follow these very simple rules, your sales and effectiveness in dealing with prospects, customers, and clients on the telephone will increase dramatically.

One
Getting Through

Whether you sell face-to-face or work primarily on the telephone, your business depends on how effectively you can talk to prospects without seeing them face-to-face, at least initially.

What do you think your customers want most from you? Let me give you five choices.

1. Contact with a capable outside salesperson.
2. Frequency and speed of product delivery.
3. Price range.
4. Range of available products.
5. Contact with a capable inside salesperson.

According to a study done by Arthur Andersen and Company way back in 1970, the number-one thing on the customer's mind was having contact with a capable and competent outside salesperson. But in 1985, the same study showed that contact with an outside salesperson was dead last, number five. In the number-one spot was a capable *inside*, phone salesperson. Today the reliance on a capable inside salesperson is even more important, and inside, consulting salespeople are even more valued. This is because more vendors are forcing you to use their technology to communicate instead of people. Have you noticed how difficult it can be to talk to someone? They would rather have you read their FAQ page.

Obviously, frequency and speed of delivery as well as a suitable range of products were still important. Also important was getting a good price, but the studies showed that your prospects are not as money-limited as they are time-limited.

Have you noticed? People and things are pulling at us from all directions, trying to entice time away from us. Chances are, you put more value on your own time than on money. Most of us will pay a huge amount of money to get convenience. You'll pay a premium to get something that will save you time. This concept is important to realize in telephone selling and customer service: what customers really want is to get things accomplished in less time. When they see a salesperson in their office, they expect to spend sixty to ninety minutes to achieve even the simplest of objectives. On the phone, they can get things accomplished in ten to twenty minutes. Granted, it's easier to communicate when we're face-to-face with each other, but if you're good on the telephone, you can accomplish far more in a shorter period of time. That also means you can make more money more quickly.

In the movie *Back to the Future,* Michael J. Fox was whisked in a futuristic time machine back to the mid-1950s. In a small hometown, he ate dinner at a home in which the father had a nice, new black and white television set. Michael made the mistake of telling this family that he had two television sets in his home in the future. The kids in the family showed strong reactions as their mouths dropped open in amazement, obviously marveling at such vast resources. Can you imagine what your grandkids would say if you told them what life was like without the internet and social media?

What if you told them that you listened to AM radio and had to park the car without radar beeping or a rear-facing camera?

Times have certainly changed, haven't they? We possess more spendable income than ever before but have less time to enjoy it.

Tom Lambert, a wholesaler with a real-estate limited partnership company based in Salt Lake City, covers six states. Getting business done in such a large territory may impress you, but it's even more phenomenal when you think he only travels two days a week. Obviously, marriages are hurt when the breadwinner travels too much, but Mr. Lambert has found a way of using the telephone so that by the time he sees someone face-to-face, he is nearly 100 percent sure that he will do business.

One stockbroker in Santa Ana, California, with the old Smith Barney earned approximately $750,000 a year, yet he saw only one-third of his clients. How could this happen? He communicated sincerity and honesty to his clients over the telephone, and they trusted him so much that they didn't need to see him in person.

A life-insurance salesperson in Toledo, Ohio, has a 100 percent closing rate. Making more than $1.2 million a year, he qualifies his prospects over the telephone so well that he rarely wastes time with a prospect who will not buy.

Research has shown that approximately 65 percent of the face-to-face appointments are with the wrong prospect. This means that more than two-thirds of the people you see are people you should not have been talking to in the first place. Now that you know this, it makes a lot of sense to treat the telephone as the best tool you can ever use to increase your business.

Now let's focus on how to approach and get through to prospects and clients. Have you ever had problems building your prospect's interest in the first few minutes? If you're like me, you've been rejected or put off, or even had prospects who wouldn't let you talk to them at all.

One thing I've learned through years of training salespeople is that most marketers, whether they're selling a product or simply trying to book an appointment, forget that the prospect or client on the other end of the telephone is human too. These salespeople concentrate so hard on the product's benefits that they lose sight of what the person on the other side of the line wants to hear.

The most important thing in approaching a prospect on the telephone is to remember that first you need to gain rapport. Second, you need to solve their problems.

One of the biggest problems with cold calling is that your call interrupts your prospect in whatever he was doing. That interruption is often less irritating if your call is the result of a referral, so you have to be more skilled in making cold calls than referral calls.

A few years ago, I hired a new phone salesperson for my business. After a few months, I realized that she wasn't making much headway. The more I taught her about my business, the worse she seemed to get.

I listened in on a few of her calls. I couldn't figure out why she was so unproductive. She sounded great to me. I didn't realize that she was talking product to her prospects the entire time. She failed to trade social amenities with them. She wasn't generating a common ground or any degree of familiarity.

People buy from people who are like them. They buy from people who develop trust with them. In making a cold call, you must develop and generate rapport more quickly than on a referral call. Here are a few steps to help you make and approach cold calls a little more effectively.

Number one: introduce yourself and your company immediately. While this may seem obvious, I've heard many salespeople introduce themselves but fail to talk about their company. This deprives your prospect of a reference point. Say, for example, "Hi, Mr. Jones. My name is Kerry Johnson with International Productivity Systems."

Probably the most important thing you can do in the first thirty seconds of a cold call is to get the prospect to respond. This initial response from the prospect is so crucial that if you talk through or at him, you'll cause him to drift off and blow you off the telephone with objections.

Use your prospect's name two or three times during the introduction. Obviously you shouldn't say, "Hi, Mr. Brown, Mr. Brown, Mr. Brown" three times in a row, but one thing you can do is say, "John Brown. Hi, Mr. Brown. My name is Kerry Johnson with International Productivity Systems." You've undoubtedly heard that your own name is music to your ears, but more importantly, a greeting afterward will cause your prospect to respond to you, thereby getting him to participate in the phone call much more quickly. Using this technique to get him to greet you afterwards is a surefire way of warming him up to you in the critical first few seconds.

Would you like to know the biggest mistake you can make in the first fifteen seconds on the telephone? Here it is. I would like you to participate in a short test with me. Take a few moments and write down three words—"How are you?"—twenty-five times on an 8½ by 11 sheet of paper. Stop reading and do it now.

Have you done it? Good. Now cross each of those "how are you's" out, and never say them again on the telephone. "How are you?" is the most plastic, phony, empty phrase you can ever use. Even if that prospect of yours is lying in bed with a 104-degree temperature, he will say, "I'm fine." Even if he is deathly ill, he'll say, "Wonderful." Then you'll say, "Oh, that's nice," and carry on.

Number two: when you talk to a prospect on the phone, make sure you give him a benefit within the first thirty seconds of the conversation. This is especially important on cold calls, because the quicker you can give that person a good reason to listen to you, the longer he's going to stay on the line, giving you a chance to solve his problems.

Here's an example. "John Brown. Hi, Mr. Brown. My name is Kerry Johnson with International Productivity Systems."

Mr. Brown will likely respond, "Hello."

"I'd like to talk to you about increasing your salespeople's overall production levels."

In other words, the quicker you can give that prospect a benefit, the quicker you'll grab his attention. In the first thirty seconds, that prospect is trying to find a reason to prevent you from getting his attention. He's talking to an associate, he's working on a project, he might even be making some telephone calls of his own. The last thing he wants to do is let you take some of his valuable time.

Have you ever had a prospect, especially during a cold call, give you an initial objection? Have you ever heard these phrases within the first thirty seconds? "I don't buy over the telephone. I'm sorry, I'm not interested. I don't have time to talk to you."

Initial objections are extremely difficult to overcome, because you haven't been able to get started, and the prospect is trying to push you out of his life. When you make a cold call and get an objection in the first thirty seconds, you need to do something quick. You need to find a way of grabbing that prospect's interest very fast.

When your prospect gives you an introductory objection, make sure that you (1) show understanding and (2) give a quick benefit.

Portray understanding and benefit, and don't falter. If that prospect senses that you're actually listening, yet are persistent and tenacious, he's much more apt to stay on the telephone with you.

For example, that prospect might say, "I don't buy over the phone." Your response should be, "I understand that you normally don't buy over the telephone. Are you interested in increasing your salespeople's production by 80 percent in eight weeks?" If at that point he says, "Tell me more about it," you should immediately present another supporting benefit, or a situation with another client in which you were able to achieve that increased production. For example: "Mr. Jones, we achieved that with one of our other clients recently. I'm not sure I can do that with your people, but I would like to ask you some questions to find out."

What if your prospect initially says, "I'm not interested"? What do you say then? "I understand you're not interested. Would you like to increase your salespeople's production by 80 percent within eight weeks?" Or he might say, "I don't have time for you." Your response would be, "I understand you don't have time. Would you like to discover how to increase your salespeople's production within eight weeks?" In each of these cases, you were showing understanding and then moving right into a quick benefit. This enables you to move on to another stage, which we'll discuss later, called *probing*.

Many salespeople make the mistake of using the "yes, but" technique. This only causes your prospect to feel even more irritated than before. For example, if he says, "I don't have time for you," the inept salesperson would say, "Yes, but do you have time to learn how to increase sales?" This only serves to push your prospect against the wall. Wouldn't it be easier to draw your prospect to you through understanding and then give a quick benefit?

What if the prospect still says no? In making cold calls, you have to realize that you should never get into a battle. Years ago, salespeople use to call on the phone at the rate of 100 to 150 calls per day. They would make call after call, trying to wrestle and argue prospects into listening to their sales pitch. Your prospects receive too many sales calls for you to do that. More importantly, if you try to wrestle each prospect to the ground, you'll soon wear yourself out. Your psychological well-being and stability are directly related to how much you enjoy making those phone calls. Don't allow yourself to experience deep rejection or let prospects abuse you if you can avoid it.

The game in cold-call sales is to find qualified and interested prospects. One sales pro trained in the stockbrokerage industry calls it "cherry picking." If you're a successful cold caller, you'll likely realize that you'll only get a few cherries out of every hour's worth of cold calls. The sales pro also says to avoid "pit picking." If a prospect is very negative initially, get off the telephone quickly. Go to your next prospect. Don't let that negative prospect depress you and ruin the rest of your day. Don't let it get to you. There's a big difference between pushing your prospects and finding a truly interested prospect.

I once trained new salespeople with an insurance company on how to get appointments. They worked on Sunday evenings making cold calls. A few of the salespeople were so serious that they took it personally when a prospect said no. They would plead with every cold call to agree to a face-to-face appointment. As you might have guessed, out of every ten phone calls, they would get eight or nine extremely negative people, whom they would try to argue into seeing them. Fifty percent of those they argued with eventually said they would see them but kept canceling appointments. If you cold-call, make sure that the prospect actually is interested and is qualified to see you. You'll save yourself a lot of grief in the long run.

The best people to help you get through to the right person in a company are the receptionists. The job of the receptionist is to help you get where you want to go. Think about this. Every single day, the receptionist in that company keeps saying, "Can I help you? Can I help you? Can I help you?" She's almost like a recording. In fact, if American society could find a way for replacing the receptionist, they would cure the boredom of a lot of these people. (But wait; they have. It's called voice mail.)

The receptionist's duties consist of saying, "Can I help you?" taking messages, writing them down, or connecting you to the proper extension. I recommend that you first introduce yourself to the receptionist. If you do this, she'll be much more helpful. She would like to know who you are. Also, before you ask for her help, make sure that you compliment her. Day in and day out, she listens to people demanding that they be connected with their target quarry. Nobody ever asks her name or inquires what she enjoys or dislikes about her job. If you really want to make points, compliment that receptionist.

Recently when I called a company executive, the receptionist said, "Can I help you?" I said, "My name is Kerry Johnson. Boy, you sound cheery. You must have just come back from a vacation."

Now this may sound frivolous and flamboyant to you, but this person has been treated like a robot for most of the day. When she hears someone truly interested in her, she's certainly not going to be flippant or curt. Then use the receptionist as a resource. After I complimented her, I said, "By the way, who is the director of sales there?"

"Oh, that's Don Jones."

"Don Jones, huh? Would you please put me through to him?"

"I'd be glad to."

The receptionist is not going to ask you, "Sir, what is this regarding?" She's going to say, "Let me put your through to him right now." She's going to say, "I'll see if he's in." If he's not at his desk, she'll probably page him for you. She's much more apt to page him or leave a message if she knows who you are. You can bet that the message will get through to him as long as you've built rapport with her.

Here's a warning: the receptionist will help you, but she doesn't have time to chat. Have you ever called a receptionist and discovered that she really doesn't want to take your message? That's because she is handling so many phone calls, she doesn't want to take the time to write something down that would cause her to be late in answering the other calls. Doing so might mean building a backlog of calls.

The secretary's job, on the other hand, is to screen and block you from getting to the decision maker. In President Ronald Reagan's administration, the person to block access to the president was his chief of staff, Donald Regan. One of the biggest problems with the Reagan administration was lack of access to the chief executive. In the minds of some White House staffers, Don Regan abused the office of chief of staff. He pushed Ronald Reagan into a kind of cocoon, which some believe shielded him from the knowledge of White House operations, such as the Iran arms scandal.

In the Donald Trump administration, the opposite was often true. Chief of Staff John Kelly tried to control the President's schedule. But often Trump's friends and those he wanted to talk to, would almost just pop in. But you can bet that the assistants you call will be very protective.

Think of a secretary as the chief of staff. Her primary job is to keep you away, routing only certain people to the executive. Every secretary has been told by her boss at least once to avoid letting salespeople through to him. The longer the secretary has been working for one boss, the more aggressive she will be at blocking you. She is paid to screen anybody whom the boss hasn't told her ahead of time to let through. She is basically the judge of her boss's time; a good secretary prioritizes her boss's time so that he can get as much done as possible.

On my staff, my secretary, Jamie, will often screen those people calling in. She has decided on her own to get the caller's name and company and then give the information to me before she transfers the phone call. This may seem fairly simplistic and obvious to you, but she will not let that caller know whether I'm in the office or not unless I say I want to talk to him.

Jamie is certainly not in a minority. Most of the secretaries that stand in your way have a script. They stay with that secretary script as closely as possible. Some things you'll hear from it are lines such as, "He's in a meeting." "He's unavailable right now." "He's out of the office." "He's away from his desk."

The most important point to remember in dealing with a secretary is if you let her stay on her script, she will block you, but if you get her off it, she may let you through. Think of a secretary as a robotlike creature. Secretaries are underpaid and overworked people. They don't like grief, and they do not crave conflict. If you short-circuit a robot, it will drop its defenses and turn itself off. Similarly, if you short-circuit a secretary by giving her a comment that she does not expect, she may also drop her guard, turn off, and let you through.

In getting through secretaries, you must have an expectant attitude. Don't say, "Is Mr. Brown in?" Make the secretary think that you and Mr. Brown are the best of friends. You'll hear from a secretary, for example, "Mr. Brown's office. May I help you?" Your response would be, "Bob Brown, please." Make that secretary think that you and Mr. Brown are on the phone together constantly and know each other well.

One technique that I use in getting through is to ask for the prospect by his first name. The secretary might say, "Mr. Brown's office." I say, "Is Bob in?" Or "Is he in?" If that secretary senses that there is a high degree of familiarity, she is much more apt to avoid blocking me, but if she thinks it's the first time you've talked to him, she'll put a screen up that only a gnat can get through.

A secretary might ask, "Who may I say is calling?" or "Who's calling?" A great response in this situation is to let that secretary know where you're from as well as giving your name. If it's in state, give the city. If it's out of state, give the state.

For example, a secretary might say, "Who may I say is calling?" In state, you would say, "Kerry Johnson in Irvine." If it's out of state, say, "Kerry Johnson in California." Sixty percent of the time, if the prospect is in, you will get through.

Recently, I called a prospect in New York. I could tell the secretary was going to be difficult by the way she answered the telephone, but I decided to try to use some of these techniques and had very good luck:

"Mr. Thomas's office."

"Is he in?"

"Who's calling?" she said, without letting me know whether he was in or not.

I said, "Kerry Johnson from California."

She said, "I'll put you right through."

You've undoubtedly heard that a great prophet is never known in his own land. For some reason in our ever shrinking society, we instantly associate a long-distance phone call with a high degree of authority and importance. You're very likely to get through if that prospect thinks that you're from another area besides his.

For example, if you're with New York Life Insurance Company, and you say, "This is Kerry Johnson calling with New York Life," if the prospect has not spoken to you before, he is very likely to think that you're trying to sell him life insurance. He may avoid taking the phone call. In many cases, when the secretary hears, "Kerry Johnson from Irvine," she'll go to the prospect and tell him who you are.

In an effort to avoid taking another step, the boss may not say, "Ask him what company he's with." He may instead say, "Put him through." You could actually tell the secretary later what company you are with.

Sixty percent of the time, indicating where you're from will get you through, but what about the other 40 percent of the time? What about those situations where the assistant is much more aggressive in her screening duties? Have you ever heard an assistant ask, "What is this regarding?" Does this put you through a cold sweat, knowing that if you tell her truthfully, she'll block you and never let you talk to the prospect? The assistant's job is to carry out directions. So simply give her what she wants. Give her a direction to carry out.

A two-step technique in getting through the 40 percent of the assistants who will try to block you is to answer their question and give an instructional directive statement. For example:

"What is this regarding?"

"This is regarding a letter I sent last week. Would you please tell him I'm on hold?"

Answer the question and give an instructional statement. You must realize that an assistant is like a trial lawyer in cross-examination. Anything you tell her will be used against you. She will go right to her boss and say something like, "It's just a salesman. Do you want me to tell him to get lost?" Or "It's not important. Would you like me cut him off?"

The secretary might say something like, "Has he requested information from you?"

"Yes, would you please tell him I'm on hold?"

For example, if you're in the financial-services business, such as stockbrokerage, life insurance, or even real estate, the secretary might say, "What is this regarding?"

Your response: "It's regarding a personal financial matter. Would you please let him know I'm waiting?"

One of the best ways to get through quickly is to send a pre-approach letter. In many cases, as I've consulted to salespeople from coast to coast, when they make cold calls, they first send a cold letter as a way to get through the secretary. When a secretary asks, "What is this regarding?" it's very easy to say to say, "It's regarding correspondence I sent to him last week" or "It's regarding the letter he received last week."

You're going to find such power in using these techniques that 98 percent of the time, you'll get through, but I have heard salespeople abuse their power in dealing with assistants. There are some unscrupulous salespeople who say things like, "It's personal," or "It's a confidential matter." I have even gotten a phone call from a female once who got through my assistant by saying, "Just tell him it's Nancy." When my secretary said can I tell him what it's regarding, she said, "It's personal." The good news is that you will probably get through to the prospect. The bad news is when a prospect gets on the telephone and finds out that it was just a ploy, he will never talk to you again.

On the other hand, if you are unable to get through to the prospect by using a pre-approach letter, you can always send a copy of the letter back to him with a handwritten note saying something like, "I've tried to get through to you, but your assistant keeps blocking me. Please contact me." Or "I've tried three times to reach you on the telephone. Please contact me." (We'll talk more about jotting notes later.)

You are probably thinking, "Kerry, snail mail was twenty years ago." I realize that you may be a millennial and don't know what letterhead looks like. But the more prevalent email is, the more it is ignored and the more unique a physical letter becomes. I open all my letters and just scan my emails. (You will also have a harder time jotting a handwritten note at the bottom of an email.)

A few years ago, I became overconfident. I had a special technique in getting through secretaries. Since I have a PhD, I'm entitled to use the term "doctor" as I introduce myself. In many cases, when I'm calling people who don't know me or know about me, if I were to say, "This is Kerry Johnson calling," they won't let me through, but if I say, "This is Dr. Kerry Johnson," it's much easier.

I always must be careful of treading that fine line between letting on that it could be a medical emergency and using the fact that "doctor" is simply my title. I called a company executive years ago whose secretary answered the telephone. I said, "Is Dan there?"

She said, "Who's calling?"

I said, "Dr. Kerry Johnson."

"I'll check if he's available." She came back to the telephone and said, "He's unavailable right now. Can he call you back?"

Because of my over aggressiveness, I said, “Can he be disturbed?” It was a referral call, but it was not important enough to disturb the man. When he got on the telephone, I said, “This is Dr. Kerry Johnson. I was referred to you by Dan Thompson, who said you might be interested in using a speaker at your next conference.”

The secretary, in transferring the message to him, had said, “It’s Dr. Kerry Johnson.” He’d gotten alarmed. He thought that his son had broken his leg or had been injured in some way. He’d interrupted his meeting and jumped on the telephone, and he was irate that I had used such tactics to get through. He told me never to call again.

Even now, some assistants ask if it’s an emergency or if I should be put through right away and interrupt a meeting. In most cases, I say, “No, no. Please have him call me back regarding Don Jones.” The moral of the story is, don’t get overconfident with your new power.

Have you ever heard an assistant say, “He’s away from his desk,” or “He’s not in his office right now”? You then left a message for him to call back.

You wasted an enormous amount of time. The assistant did not say that he was out of the building or that he was at lunch. What she did say was that he was not at his desk. He could have been in the hallway, in the restroom, or maybe even three or four feet away from his desk. You allowed the assistant to be lazy and avoid searching the prospect out. Push them to connect him on the telephone with you.

How about voice mails? Do 90 percent of your voice mails never get returned? The answer is to not leave them in the first place. Receptionists transfer you to voice mail immediately. If your prospect isn’t sitting in front of his phone waiting for your call, he won’t return your messages. Unoccupied time not on the phone is about

5 percent. For example, I coach clients nearly every morning. The only time I am at my desk and not on the phone. is between thirty-six and forty minutes past the hour. If you don't call during this four-minute window, you will get my voice mail.

How do you get past voice mail? Don't leave long messages on voice mail. Leave only your name and possibly your company, but that is it. Ask the receptionist if your prospect is in the building. They will automatically put you through to voice mail. Then dial "0" or call back. This will work 75 percent of the time. If you can talk to your prospect directly, you will have an 80 percent greater chance of advancing your sales process.

Here are more ideas for getting the prospect on the phone. When you hear, "He's away from his desk, ask instead, "Can he be paged? Would you please page him? This is Dr. Kerry Johnson." Don't depend on the prospect returning your phone call. If it's a new prospect, in many cases you'll have difficulty getting a phone call returned. Have you ever heard, "He's unavailable now. He's on another telephone call. May I take a message"? Again, if you say yes and give her your phone number, you've just wasted your time and possibly struck out before entering the batter's box.

From now on, if your prospect is on another line, say, "Please let him know I'm holding." That prospect may simply be chatting with a friend. He can often wrap up a conversation in fifteen to thirty seconds, making himself available to you. But it's crucial that you instruct the assistant to tell the prospect that you're on hold. If the secretary says she has no way of letting him know, she's at the switchboard, or his office door is closed, don't stay on hold. You'll be there forever.

On the other hand, what if he truly is unavailable? The door is closed, he's in a meeting, or he's out of the building. How do you call back a second time? Many telemarketing experts have advised never to leave your name or have the prospect call back. If, for example, you're selling car-alarm systems, when the prospect calls back and finds out what kind of company he's calling, he's likely to hang up before you get on the telephone.

On the other hand, if you think that it's better for you to call back rather than receive a return call, make sure that you at least leave your name. Leaving your name with a secretary saying that you'll call back is the kind of strategy that Madison Avenue is built on. You've just advertised who you are. If you leave your name and call a second time, the prospect is much more inclined to accept your phone call. He has a little bit better idea of who you are because he remembered your name from your previous call.

If you must ask the prospect to return your call, remember to keep his file handy. Many telemarketers call fifty to 100 prospects every day. Stockbrokers, for example, call so many people that they forget who they called. When the prospect calls back, they're busy fumbling saying things like, "Well, sir, um—can you tell me why I called? Who's your company? Where are you from?"

Meanwhile, they're busy scrambling through their files to find exactly why they called in the first place. This is extremely tacky and will very likely make you lose a prospect who may have been interested.

I made this mistake years ago, when I was calling twenty to thirty prospects per day. Sometimes a prospect would call back three or four days later. I would completely forget who they were. At first, I put them into my database. When they said who they were, I had to type the name and sort through all the Smiths and read the notes. Even a five-second wait will kill your sales. You and I will both hang up on a telemarketer who makes us wait.

I developed a low-tech system that was very effective in helping me jog my memory. At that time, I didn't have a secretary, so it was very important for me to have his name and the reason I called at the tip of my tongue. I went down to a stationery store and bought a whiteboard that I could write on with grease pencil. I would simply write the prospect's name and his company with a grease pencil, as well as the dates I tried to call.

After every five days, I would cross the people off the board who had returned my phone call. This allowed me to look at the board and quickly determine who that person was. This also helped me avoid going through stacks or files to find out who he was.

Is your market physicians or medical specialists? When you're prospecting a physician, dentist, or health practitioner, you'll find out that they're extremely difficult to contact. The assistant and receptionist are often one and the same. She's very likely to say, "He's with a patient and can't be disturbed." One of the few responses that you can give is to simply say, "I'm Kerry Johnson, and when should I call back?"

I once called a physician assistant and said, "When should I call back?" The receptionist said, "Never. I'll have him call you."

I said, "I'm tough to reach. When would you recommend I call back?"

"He's always with patients."

Among the few times you can reach a doctor are in the morning, when he's leaving or coming back from lunch, or when he's about to go to his hospital for rounds. In most cases, if you can catch him during one of those times, you'll be able to get through. It is rare that a physician will return your phone call. Even their patients have extreme difficulty getting them to return calls.

In fact, there is so much difficulty in getting past a secretary that you might as well bypass her. I once heard a salesperson solve this problem by saying to the secretary, "Gee, you really work hard, don't you? You must work twelve hours a day."

The secretary said, "No, just eight hours a day, 9:00 to 5:00."

The salesman thought, "Good." He was thinking, "I'm going to call before 9:00 and after 5:00 when you're not there."

Chances are that the doctor will be there after 5:00 doing paperwork or studying, just as that businessperson will likely be there until 6:00. Don't forget that chances are your prospect will work past 5:00, long after the secretary goes home.

Have you ever had a problem playing telephone tag? This is one of the biggest problems of doing business on the telephone. You call him. He eventually calls you back. You're not in. You call him again; he's not in. He calls you, and you throw up your arms wondering if you're ever going to be able to get the chance to run your business appropriately. Phone tag is becoming a bigger and bigger problem as more and more of us decide we're going to save time and do business directly on the telephone.

A good tip in helping your prospect get through to you when he calls back is to ask his assistant to call between certain hours. For example, "Please have Mr. Jones call between 3:00 and 5:00 tomorrow." Or "Please have him call me back in the next ninety minutes or before 5:00."

If you give your prospect definite time parameters in which to call you back, he is much more likely to call. If you simply leave a message saying, "Please have him call Kerry Johnson," and leave your phone number, you are in effect saying, "There's no rush." What happens in your business when you sense that there's no rush? You guessed it. It never gets done.

If you're like me, you often have difficulty getting people to call back whom you have spoken to before. When calling a new prospect, you often don't want to leave a message saying what the call is regarding. It could be unlikely that he will call back, but on a follow-up call, you want the client to call back as soon as possible.

Sometime ago, I had had it with clients not calling back. I became so irritated that I nearly blew my cool and wrote letters to these people saying, "I don't want your business. Don't call me back either." Sometimes we would call three or four times trying to get a simple yes or no response.

I then decided to try an experiment. I left a message for the client, left my phone number, when to call back, but also exactly what I wanted to know. The message read something like, "Please have him call me back regarding the October 14 agreement." Or "Please have him call me back regarding the Centennial partnership." The more specific you can make the message, the more likely you are to get information.

One of the worst problems in telemarking and telesales and doing business on the telephone is simply not to get any response. If you're like me, a no is better than no response. Isn't bad breath better than no breath at all?

When my staff started leaving very specific messages for our clients exactly what they wanted to know, suddenly we were getting callbacks within hours. Suddenly people were calling back that we'd called two or three times, even if they didn't have any information.

The Three-Call Script

Many people just won't return your phone calls no matter how often you call. Most will ignore more than three attempts. But you have to make the attempts. The answer lies in what you do after the three calls.

The first time you call, leave a message to call you back regarding a specific goal for them. The second time you call, let them know you missed them on the last call and that you hope they are receiving these messages.

For the third phone message needs to be the same script as below. Don't forget: if someone doesn't call back in three tries, they probably won't ever call you back. If you keep calling, you will let them waste your time. That is worse than hearing a no.

If you use this script in an email, letter, or fax to them, you will get a response 80 percent of the time. Remember that a no is better than no response.

THE THIRD CALL

> Hi ————
>
> I've been trying to get in touch with you.
>
> We have been working on the three items you wanted:
>
> 1.
>
> 2.
>
> 3.
>
> I have left messages on ———— and on ———— but I haven't heard back.
>
> The reason I'm calling is to be responsive to my clients, but I don't want to spin your wheels or waste your time by pestering you. So please get back to me even if just to say, "Take a hike!" I look forward to hearing from you.

Below are some screen shots that will help you use this script using texts.

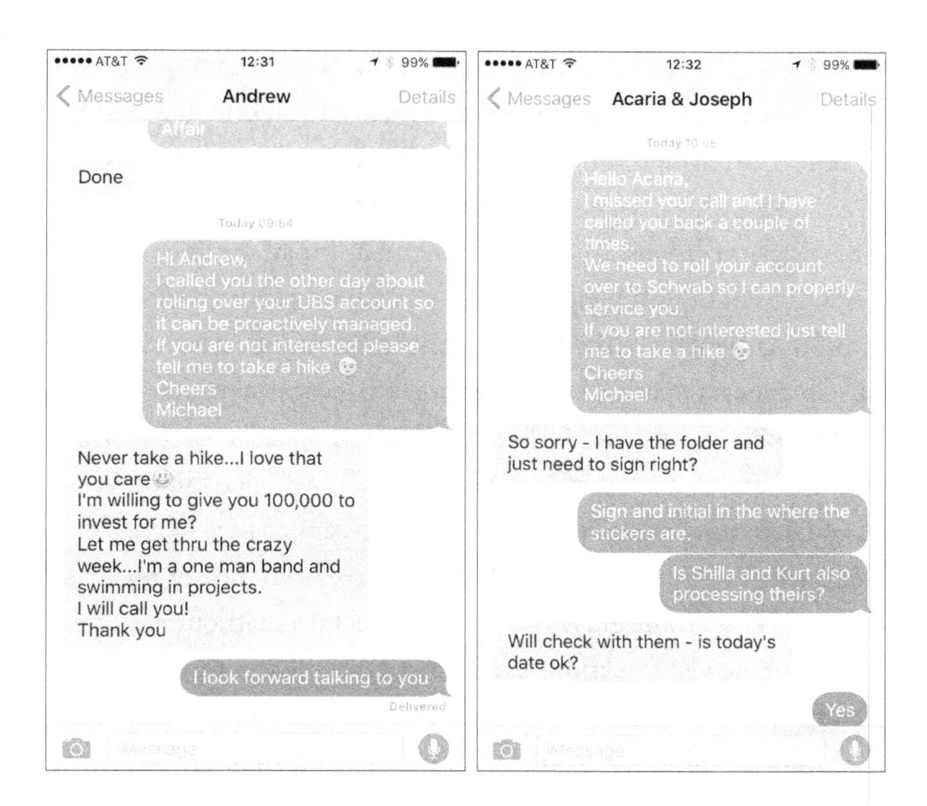

The Focal Screen

Has your prospect or client ever said, "Let me think about it" soon before they go radio-silent?

My coaching client Andrew worked with a new prospect for a few weeks. After he had presented a financial plan, the prospect wouldn't answer phone calls or emails. One theory is that the prospect decided not to implement Andrew's ideas and didn't answer his calls. A better theory is that the prospect forgot the solutions and lost a sense of any urgency, causing procrastination.

There is a better way to get both your prospects and clients to implement your suggestions and stop stalling. The answer is the *focal screen*. You have probably heard how porous memory is. We forget 70 percent of what we see and hear within one day, and 90 percent in three days. Those over fifty-five years old remember even less. That is a major reason why clients don't respond immediately to your calls and emails. They only remember broad outlines of what you spoke about. But people buy based on emotion even more than on product benefits. Emails don't convey the emotion necessary to cause prospects to act. The answer lies in the focal screen.

The Life Insurance Marketing Research Association (LIMRA) reports that if one need is uncovered, there is a 36 percent of a sale. If two needs are discovered, there is a 56 percent chance of business. If you can listen for three needs, a 92 percent chance of business appears. New producers try to sell the brochure without really listening for needs; the more experienced sort listen to needs that correspond to what their skill set can find solutions to. But most producers are also cognizant of how much information the client can process.

Thus if you can collect and present solutions based on three needs, a sale occurs 92 percent of the time. Why three needs? Human memory is coded in engrams or chunks of information. (The Internet's packet design is close to how memory works in the brain.) We can remember 3+/-2 pieces of information. The most brilliant recall more, and those paying less attention remember less. Back in the 1950s, phone numbers were alphanumerically coded, such as Merrimac 2-3397 and Columbia 6-2219. Today, they are coded in 3+/-1 digit blocks. These are area code, local prefix and four-digit identifiers such at 714-368-3650 (my phone).

Let's prove this theory. Read the following ten numbers to a colleague or friend over forty years old. (Younger folks remember more.) Don't let them write the numbers down.

22	35
67	26
83	91
52	43
74	61

After the last number, ask them to count down out loud from 100 to 95. Then ask them to recite the numbers they remember. Their memory will range from one to five, but it will never be more than that.

Did you also notice that they remembered the first and last few numbers? This is called the *primacy-recency effect*. Your client will remember more in the beginning and the end than in the middle.

The point of all this business psychology is that if you can listen for, and limit your presentation, to three needs and solutions, your closing ratio will increase.

Use the Three Needs

When you want to get a response from a radio-silent prospect, focus on their three needs. When my client Andrew tries to reconnect with clients, he now calls or writes:

Hi, Tom. When we last spoke, you were concerned with:

1. Running out of money. You want to make sure you don't end up being a greeter at Walmart.
2. Volatility. You said the ups and downs are pretty scary.
3. Taxes in retirement. You are nervous that taxes will keep increasing as the government creates massive deficits.

If these are no longer important to you, please let me know.

If you focus on the client's three needs, you will get a much faster response.

Sample Scripts

The idea seems to be that your prospect or client will respond much more quickly if he knows exactly what you want than if you only leave your name. Here are some examples of the various techniques we discussed on getting through assistants.

ASSISTANT: Mr. Brown's office. May I help you?

KERRY: Yes, is Bob in?

ASSISTANT: May I ask who's calling?

KERRY: This is Kerry Johnson from Santa Ana. Is he in?

ASSISTANT: What company are you with, sir?

KERRY: I'm with International Productivity Systems. May I speak to him?

ASSISTANT: Yes. One moment, please.

ASSISTANT: Good afternoon. Don Jones's office.

KERRY: Hi. Is Don in?

ASSISTANT: Yes, he is. May I ask who's speaking?

KERRY: Yes, this is Kerry Johnson in Santa Ana. Can I speak to him?

ASSISTANT: Sure. What is this regarding?

KERRY: It's regarding a personal financial matter. Please tell him I'm holding.

ASSISTANT: All right. Hold on, please.

ASSISTANT: Good afternoon. Mr. Butler's office.

KERRY: Hi, is Jim there?

ASSISTANT: Who may I say is calling?

KERRY: This is Kerry Johnson from California. Is he in?
ASSISTANT: I'm sorry, Mr. Johnson. He's away from his desk right now. May I take a message?
KERRY: Is he in the building?
ASSISTANT: I believe he is.
KERRY: Would you page him for me?
ASSISTANT: I'll try.

ASSISTANT: Mr. Thomas's office.
KERRY: Is Bob in?
ASSISTANT: Yes, but he's in a meeting.
KERRY: When do you expect him to be free?
ASSISTANT: About 2:30.
KERRY: Please tell him that Kerry Johnson with International Productivity Systems in Santa Ana called. I'll call back at 2:30 p.m. today. Would you let him know I'll be calling back then?
ASSISTANT: OK, I sure will.

Two

The Power of Referrals

It has long been said that cold calls are important, but you should only have to make them when you are new to sales. The definition of a great salesperson is one who knows how to make cold calls but never has to. The best producers are so good at getting referrals that they have an almost endless supply of new prospects.

If you've been selling for very long, you undoubtedly have recognized the value of a good referral. Unlike with a cold call, your new prospect almost feels compelled to talk to you because of the strength of the relationship with the person referring you to him. In many cases, business is done almost exclusively on referral. If your closing rate on getting appointments on cold calls is two out of ten, referrals will bump it up to eight or nine out of ten. The most important thing to realize about referrals is to qualify your prospect well enough to determine if you want to see him, not whether he wants to see you.

Through this chapter, you'll learn techniques on how to use and get referrals, but more importantly, you'll learn how to play on the strength of that referral and generate business for yourself.

The traditional way to obtain referrals is to ask existing clients to give you names of people they know are prequalified. For example, "Mr. Jones, you and I have been doing business for a couple of years now. I would like you to give me five people whom you know, respect, have money to invest, and would be willing to talk to me about the kind of service much like I've provided for you."

You should ask for a specific number, not just for "some" referrals. This pushes your client to try to think about three or more, hopefully even five, people they know would be candidates. Otherwise the client will give you only one or two. Rarely will the client give you more referrals than you ask for. If your client says, "I can't think of anybody," simply restate the same request you made in the first place.

Here's an important rule. Make sure that when you ask for a referral, it's part of the closing sequence. If you sign contracts, draw documents, or actually receive payment, make sure that before that person actually signs on the dotted line for your product, you get those names. As soon as he pays for the service or you shake hands, he's inclined to leave. He's busy, just like you. He will rarely want to sit around and chat, but if you make getting referrals part of the sales cycle, your client will think it's part of doing business with you. He is *supposed* to give you referrals.

The interesting corollary is that a referral usually produces more referrals. When a client who is referred buys, you will get more referrals from that client.

Make sure that you always find out something about that referral personally. Is he a tennis player? Does he play golf? Does he bowl? How big is his family? What are his associations and affiliations? Which college did he go to? The more you can find out about that prospect personally, the more likely the new prospect is to realize the strength of the referral and see that you are truly a friend of a friend.

When you call the referral, possibly the most important information you can have about him is what you know about his personal life. This will help you generate rapport. With rapport, you will develop a relationship; without rapport, you will only develop a contact. Contacts don't buy, but relationships do.

As you might have guessed by now, referrals are not like good cheese or old wine. They do not improve with age. If you desire to increase your production by utilizing referrals, make sure to contact that referral within seven days after you receive it. You have already realized that it's really not about how long after you get a referral that you call; it's about much you remember about the referral and the client. If you wait too long, you'll forget the nuances about the client and the referral, and your credibility will be diminished.

Once you've decided to make that phone call, here's a great way to approach the contact. Use the three-step technique, which I call *approach, purpose, rapport.* The prospect recognizes, number one, that the referral is important, but he has a bigger need to protect his time. He also wants to make sure that how he uses his time is beneficial to himself and his company. Using a referral will build you a bridge. This is the *approach.*

Number two: the prospect wants you to state the *purpose* for which you're calling so that he can attach value to what you have to offer. After that is number three: the *rapport* stage. This is where the real selling takes place. This is where you give the prospect a chance to get to know you.

The introduction, purpose, rapport technique might go like this.

"Mr. Jones? Hi, Mr. Jones. This is Kerry Johnson. I'm a sales trainer from Southern California. Ben Thomas, a friend of yours, gave me your name and thought you might be interested in talking to me about getting sales production up among your associates. By the way, Ben tells me you're quite a golfer. It's hard to believe that anybody playing golf these days can actually play scratch golf with absolutely no handicap. How do you do it?"

Obviously that prospect is going to make comments between those sentences, but you have introduced yourself, stated who you are, why you called, and who referred you. Afterward you can try to find out a little more about the prospect. With this technique, the chances of getting blown off the telephone are practically nil, because not only did you impart the referral's name, but you also know enough about the prospect personally and professionally to show that you invested time in finding out something about him. Your prospect will be impressed by you; even if he's not interested in your product, he'll stay on the telephone and chat with you about his golf game.

Another technique to use is to tell the prospect that the referring client asked you to call.

"Mr. Jones, Ben Thomas asked me to talk to you. I'm a sales trainer in Southern California. After I worked with Ben, he told me that you would likely be interested in finding out more about the techniques I shared with him for increasing overall production."

At this point, I have told the prospect that the referral source asked me to call. Obviously he will have a couple of comments. He will probably say:

"Well, I don't know if I need you or not. I'm not sure I'm interested. Can you tell me more?"

At this stage, you go directly into rapport.

"By the way, Ben tells me you're a great golfer. Just out of curiosity, Ben told me you were a scratch golfer. Is that really true? It's pretty incredible."

It's imperative to develop rapid rapport before you say much more about your product or service. Play the referral up to the hilt. Portray yourself as a friend of a friend.

Also with a referral, remember to get on a first-name basis as rapidly as possible:

"Mr. Bob Jones, my name is Kerry Johnson. Ben Thomas asked me to chat with you. He has been a client of mine for a couple of years and thought that you might be interested in using a sales trainer for increasing your company's overall production. By the way, Bob, he tells me that you're an excellent golfer. Is that true?"

It's a great idea to get on a first-name basis with a prospect as soon as possible, whether it's a cold call or a referral call, but especially on referrals. You'll pick up valuable points, because it will suddenly become a friendship rather than a cold referral call.

Some millennials will call the prospect by their first name immediately. That is a mistake. Baby boomers and even Gen Xers still want you to show respect in the beginning of a relationship. They may turn off if you become too familiar too fast.

Here is an example of dealing with referrals.

KERRY: Hi, Ms. Smith, my name is Kerry Johnson, with International Productivity Systems.

PROSPECT: Hello.

KERRY: I think you and I have a mutual friend in Fran Coppell. Fran tells me she plays tennis with you every week. How often do you play, by the way?

PROSPECT: Well, I try to play at least three times a week. Fran has an exceptional game.

KERRY: She says you have a great backhand as well.

PROSPECT: Well, thank you.

KERRY: Yes. Fran is a client of mine, and we've been involved in increasing her wealth through exceptional investments. I'd like to meet with you and discuss what we've been doing and see if they might work for you as well. Are you free for lunch tomorrow, by the way?

PROSPECT: Well, let me check my calendar. Hold on a second.

KERRY: OK.

PROSPECT: Well, that looks just fine.

KERRY: How about Mimi's at 12 noon? Is that all right with you?

PROSPECT: That would be wonderful.

KERRY: Great. I'll see you then.

REFERRED LEAD: OK, see you then.

Here is an example of how to gain referrals:

KERRY: Dennis, you've been a client of mine for a couple of years and a pretty good friend. In order to make my business grow, I need referrals to people as successful as you are.

DENNIS: Yes.

KERRY: I'd like the names of maybe five people you know and respect who would benefit from a service such as that I've provided for the last couple of years.

DENNIS: Well, Kerry, it might be pretty tough right now to think of anybody. I don't know.

KERRY: That's OK, Dennis. Take your time. Just people you know, respect, and would benefit from my service.

DENNIS: Well, let me think for just a moment. You know, there is one gentleman that I think–he's an old friend of mine. I've known him for ten years, and I think that he might be a pretty good one to contact. His name is Dan Rogers. Do you need his phone number?

KERRY: Sure do. Do you have it?

DENNIS: Sure. It's 645-3231.

KERRY: By the way, is there anything that you know about him, like, does he play tennis or golf, or is there anything he enjoys doing socially?

DENNIS: He's crazy about skiing.

KERRY: Really?

DENNIS: Oh, yes. He loves it.

KERRY: Anybody else you have?

DENNIS: Well, let me think for a second. You know, I guess Paul might be able to use that too.

Do you leave money on the table when you're prospecting? Maybe you think you never do, but you are probably guilty of leaving business where you should be getting some. That equals lost commissions, with money left on the table.

When you make cold calls, you're hard at work. They are difficult to make. Chances are you'll make one or two appointments or sales from every ten phone calls, if you're good, but you may never have r tried to build a referral base from clients before.

You don't need a satisfied customer to get a referral. It's likely that your referral prospect will never call your customer or client anyway. So why not jump directly in? You can even ask a negative cold-call prospect for referral, whether he likes you or not.

If your prospect says no, he isn't rejecting you personally. He's rejecting how beneficial he thinks your product or service is to him. One of the most difficult things salespeople have to realize is to detach themselves from the product. It's not you he dislikes. It's the way the product was presented and the value the prospect puts into that presentation of benefits.

When the prospect says no to you, it's a wasted call, right? Probably not. Why not turn a bad call or a negative prospect into a productive one? Have you ever asked a cold-call prospect who said no to your product for a referral? Twenty-five percent of the time he'll give you a referral even if he didn't like your product. Here's how it works.

KERRY: Mr. Jones, my name is Kerry Johnson with International Productivity Systems. Hi. We're working with a lot of businesses like yours in Santa Ana in an effort to increase sales production. How many salespeople do you have?

PROSPECT: I'm not interested.

KERRY: I understand you're not interested. One of your competitors, Rental Systems, used my firm and realized a 71 percent increase in sales in six weeks. I'd like to make an appointment with you next week to show you how they did it.

PROSPECT: I'm still not interested.

KERRY: OK, Mr. Jones, I understand. Do you know any company owners or sales managers who might be interested in a sales increase like this?

One of two things will happen. Either the prospect doesn't feel comfortable with giving you names because he knows nothing about you, or he will give you a name. In fact, research has shown that only 30 percent of those people who have said no to you on the telephone will avoid giving you referrals.

You must get over the idea that they're rejecting you. They're not. They're rejecting the product. They probably like you. They probably respect you for making that phone call and wish their salespeople were as persistent as you. They may believe that your service could be appropriate for someone else if not for them.

The second thing that could happen is this:

PROSPECT: Hmm, let's see. There's a couple of guys I know from my Rotary club who are business owners. They always tell me how bad their salespeople are. I bet they could use you.

KERRY: Would you mind if I used your name only to say that you and I talked on the telephone?

PROSPECT: Well, just if you say that, I guess it's OK.

KERRY: Do you know their phone numbers?

If you think this is ridiculous, try it. It will make you lots of money. People are often willing to help you even if they've rejected you. But you must be nice to them, and they must like you personally.

Even a referral from a prospect who said no is better than making a cold call. The only stipulation is that the prospect needs to know the person who gave the referral to you. If they don't, it's just like a cold call.

Years ago, I prospected the realty company RE/MAX. I talked to a sales manager on a cold call who told me he wasn't interested. He didn't know me, and they didn't have any meetings for which they could use a speaker like me. I told him how much I appreciated his candor and asked if he knew any other RE/MAX regional managers who might benefit from a speaker on sales psychology.

He spent a few seconds thinking about it and gave me the names of five qualified regional managers plus their telephone numbers. He told me a little bit about each of these people, the size of their families, how big their houses were—anything that might have been of interest to me. I told him how much I appreciated those referrals.

I immediately called those five referred prospects and booked two of them, largely from the strength of the person who gave them to me. You are wasting money unless you use every opportunity to gain referrals.

How To Get Massive Amounts of Referrals

Would you like to get 100 to 500 referrals just from one source? In this section, I'll give you probably the single most important tool that built my business. I used a network list. One of the best ways of finding out which prospects you want to get is to pre-qualify those people by gaining access to an association or an affiliation of people belonging to a common group.

These lists of people are published and are likely to be available from associations like Rotary, Kiwanis, insurance associations, employers' associations, even performing-arts supporters. You should choose a list after you've qualified it to make sure it's the best list possible.

The best way to call on a list is to avoid starting with the As. Always start with the Zs at the end of the list. Every salesperson in the country starts with the As and goes to the Bs, Cs, Ds, and so on. Most of the time they hit the D's and give up. They go from the Addlemans to the Barkleys to the Cannons to the Dentons. Do you know what happens when you start with the As? You got it. You get rejected.

Guess who gets called the most. The As. Guess who will get rejected? You will. Which is why you should start with the Zs and work from back to forward or even from middle to back.

I have a very close tennis friend whose name is Addleman. One day while we were having a Coke together, he said that he gets called by stockbrokers four times a week. I was shocked. I had no idea he was so popular. He wasn't all that wealthy, but apparently he was on a list. He even told me he had a three-by-five card above his telephone to let a visitor know exactly what to say to the salesman in case he wasn't there. If you want to get rejected, start with the As. If you want a prospect who may book an appointment with you, start with the Zs.

A great way to use a list is to develop a rating system from A to D, or from one to four. You learned from grammar school that an A is top-notch. An "A" is an interested prospect who might buy right there, right then, and has a need. A "B" is an individual who is interested but does not have a pressing need. A "C" may be an individual who is interested, but not right now. You can call him back in six months. A "D" is that prospect on the list who basically says to you, "Take a hike, buddy."

If you're making steady cold calls, you should be calling prospects at the rate of at least one person every two to three minutes. If that individual is a "D," get off the telephone. Don't argue with him. If you can't get past the initial objections, don't allow your prospect to bring you down by telling you how much he dislikes having you call him.

Here's a rule of thumb. If at least 10 percent of the prospects you call per hour from a list are not "A"s, get another list. If less than 10 percent of these people are interested and have a need, put that list into a manila envelope and mail it to your competition. Mark the cover with big block letters: "HOT PROSPECTS." Let them waste time making call after call, not you.

You have probably heard that approximately 20 percent of your prospects give you about 80 percent of your business. Unfortunately, salespeople spend about 80 percent of the time on 20 percent of the prospects. They are unqualified but nice to talk to. So to avoid being rejected, they talk too long to these unqualified individuals. In other words, don't spend an inordinate amount of time with prospects who love to talk but won't buy.

I got started by speaking at local associations of groups I wanted to do business with. Years ago, I was a consultant trying to find a way to get more consulting business. One way a consultant develops a reputation is by speaking in front of groups. This is precisely what I did.

I spoke to a few sales groups, trying to showcase my work as a sales trainer. I was twenty-five years old and wet behind the ears. I didn't know all that much. I spent a year as a smiling and dialing stockbroker, but didn't know many of the ins and outs of being a professional salesperson. That, as you know, takes years and years of experience to develop.

I got lucky one day. One of my clients gave me a list of local sales associations within the state association he belonged to. I looked over it and asked if I could use his name. Since he was on the board of trustees, he said, "Fine. Do the best you can."

Since these local association chapters were in California, I immediately went to the middle of the list in Modesto, California. I called the one association exec and said,

"Floyd Nolan, on the board of trustees for the state association, gave me your name."

These local presidents often didn't know who Floyd Nolan was, but by using his name, even with the very large list, I was able to get much better results than with a cold call. I was able to make a connection the prospect recognized, and thereby got to speak to the group. I still had to sell myself, but I had a first entrée from a referral the prospect recognized (or at least thought he should recognize). I virtually created a sale.

Now you're probably thinking, "How do I get access to a list, Kerry?" It's simple. Chances are, your prospects each belong to ten associations. Simply write down all the characteristics of a qualified prospect. Is he forty years of age? Does he make over $150,000 a year? Does he have employees? Does he have cloud-based servers? What makes that person qualified for you?

Then call a couple of your clients who fit that category and ask them what associations they belong to. When they tell you, ask them for a directory. Ask your client if you can use his name and make calls to all the members of that association. You'll be surprised at how many cherries or "A" prospects per hour you'll generate from a strong referral given by an association colleague.

Here's something you might say to a member of an association. Taking for granted that you have a referral name from a member, here's an example of what may work.

"Mr. Smith, Don Smith? Hi, my name is Kerry Johnson, Mr. Smith. I have a company called International Productivity Systems, which specializes in increasing sales production for companies such as yours. I recently was able to work with Fred Jones of Simtax Computer Systems. Fred is a member of your National Organization of Computer Owners. Fred said your company may benefit from my services. I'd like to meet with you to determine whether I might contribute to increasing your company's sales."

The warm association referral is a little weaker than a personal one. You don't know if the prospect goes bowling. You don't know what kind of car he drives. Nonetheless, the connection is made to someone he thinks he should know who belongs to the same association he does. This is enough to get you in the door. Then the real selling job starts.

Three

Following Up

Are you good at following up? Even the best telephone salespeople, who are often effective throughout 90 percent of the sales process, leave 10 percent hanging, thereby losing the sale. It's all about follow-up.

Most of your prospects on the telephone, unless you make an appointment to see them face-to-face, will say, "Send me something." This is often a camouflage screen to get you off the telephone. The individual could just be a "C" prospect wanting information out of curiosity, never intending to buy.

Here's a quick way to qualify a prospect to determine whether or not he is trying to blow you off the telephone with a request for written information. Use your own words, but say something like this.

"Mr. Prospect, I would love to send you something, but I don't want to waste your time. Can I ask a few questions first?" You want to send information, but you also don't want to waste your own time. If he says, "Yes," then you have a qualified prospect to spend time on. If he says, "No, thank you very much," consider him a "D" prospect, and move on.

Recently a referred lead asked me to send her something. I said, "Of course," but I didn't know what to send. I asked if I could ask some questions first. After a few minutes I discovered she was totally unqualified and would have wasted my time. She was only trying to get me off the phone. Don't waste your time on "D" prospects. Ask questions first. Qualify.

Timing

The best way to follow up is within two to four days after your prospect receives the written correspondence. If your business is such that you must snail-mail things out, make sure that you don't go more than seven days without following up. As I mentioned before, 90 percent of what we see and hear as human beings will be forgotten within three days. Ninety-five percent will be forgotten within seven days. Ninety-eight percent of what we see and hear is forgotten within one year. In other words, long-term memory includes only 2 percent of the information that we see and hear. It should make very good sense that you must follow up with a prospect, worst case, within seven days after you talk to him. This assumes the mail will get to him within three or four days. If you used email, follow up after two days at a maximum.

Have you ever sent information and found that the prospect hasn't read it? When you call and say, "Did you get my material?" he said, "I got it, but I haven't had time to look it over yet."

A computer salesperson had a problem like this. He would generate a prospect's interest and send a gorgeous, beautiful, four-color brochure. The brochures must have been expensive. Brochures and other promotional information are often sizable investments.

Out of frustration one day, he took a brochure, tore it up, and bent the pictures. He mutilated the brochure and sent it to a new prospect with a cover letter saying, "I hope you look over the material." A week later, he called the prospect back and asked if he had received the material.

The prospect said, "You know, I spent a whole half hour looking through this brochure you sent, and it was difficult for me to get through this thing. I had to straighten out the pictures and even lay books on top of it to get a better idea of what the pictures looked like."

The light bubble went on in this salesman's head. Ding. They're not reading something that's prepared in a nice, neat, and organized way. They will read something that's disorganized, mutilated. It will generate more attention. It's called the *mutilation principle*.

If you send physical correspondence, it's obviously a great idea to send a cover letter. But if you send anything else out, make sure you write in red ink on that brochure or put a yellow canary Post-it note with a few words saying, "Read this part," or "This is important," or circle things in red or blue that are especially important for him to look at.

Don't assume that your prospect is a bookworm. When you grab his attention by marking the item, he's much more apt to see and understand what you want him to see. It is even a great idea to handwrite a short note at the bottom of your cover letter. Maybe do a PS saying, "It was great talking to you. I'll follow up and talk to you on the telephone a week from today."

Fifty years ago, when a businessperson received a handwritten note, he was impressed. He received something that the sender had taken a lot of time preparing. These days it's even more impressive. We are so time-compressed that few folks take the time to jot a handwritten note. I'm not saying that you can't type a cover letter to all your prospects. I am saying that you should try to let your prospect know what is important by marking up the prepared letter and materials.

Steps to a Perfect Follow-up

When you do follow up, make sure you follow the usual steps of identifying yourself with the prospect. But first generate rapport. Now you know how to do this.

"John, how was your week? Have you been busy lately?" Now you know that you should never say, "How are you?" but should think of something else to say such as, "How's your day going?" Second, remind him of your last conversation:

"John, when we last spoke, you wanted me to send you some information about our 3X90D injection system."

Also requalify that prospect. If he has told you the price was important, remind him of that. If he tells you the delivery was important, remind him of that too.

"Mr. Prospect, when we last talked, you told me that you wanted me to send some information to determine whether we could be competitive with your current supplier."

Don't say to your prospect, "Did you get my information? Did you read it?" Assume they have read it. Don't ask. There's a good reason for this. If you say, "Did you read the literature that I sent you?" he automatically has a built-in objection to stall you. He can simply say, "Well, to tell you the truth, no, I really haven't had a chance to read it. Could you call me back in a few days?" But, if you say, "Did you get it?" chances are he did. Possibly he's not a reader. There's a good chance that he wants to hear about it from you. He doesn't even want to look at what you sent him.

If your prospect does stall you, though, requalify him. "John, are you still interested in this? Is the 10 percent discount below your current supplier still important to you?" Obviously, if that prospect says, "Well, really, no," then you've wasted one phone call. Don't waste any more.

If you've been selling very long, you've probably had to call a prospect back more than once. The most frustrating thing to me in my career is calling a prospect back time and time again to find that he's not in. He hasn't done what he said he would do, or he's away from the office traveling someplace.

We use a very effective technique in my company. I hope it works for you: Never call a prospect back after three tries. Assume that the prospect is not interested or not motivated enough to put you on his top priority list.

If that prospect is not in the first time, leave a very specific phone message: "Mr. Jones, I want to talk to you about a decision on the 3DSX injection system." If you call him a second time, let that secretary know that it is the second time you've called. Ask her to put on the message slip that you called two times, and leave the same specific message.

On the third try, take out the last piece of correspondence or letter you've written to him. Write a handwritten note at the bottom of a copy of that correspondence. For example, "Mr. Prospect, I've called you three times. I would like to find out whether you're interested in the 3DSX injection system. I also would like to know whether you're still interested in saving 10 percent below your current supplier, as we discussed."

As I said before, in using the three-call script, you can send an email outlining the three needs. But a handwritten note is always better. You will find that 65 percent of these people will call you back. Often you'll find prospects who are not courteous enough to return phone calls, but they will respond to something in writing—possibly because they don't want to engage with you on the phone. But at least they've gotten back to you.

Lastly, here's a very good point. Make sure that whenever you send a letter to a prospect, when a referral is involved, copy the letter to the referral source. You have a built-in salesperson there. If your client sees your prospect again, he will mention you. "John, did you get a chance to talk to Kerry at International Productivity Systems? He did a great job for us. I hope you get a chance to see him."

If your prospect or client realizes that you followed up with his referral, he's very likely to give you more referrals. If you copy a letter regarding what you said to your prospect, they will help you sell the business.

Four

Read the Script

Have you ever wondered why some people seem extremely smooth on the telephone while others sound as if they've just woken up? If you think it's simply a natural attribute or something in the genes, you're mistaken. The ones who are smoother are very likely those who are using a script while talking to you on the telephone.

Telephone selling is one of the very few verbal means of contact where you can actually use a cheat sheet or a script. If you're good at using a script, your prospect will never know. If you're bad, you'll sound like a scratched record.

I was recently called by a phone salesperson requesting a donation for my alumni association. This woman was obviously young and inexperienced. She sounded as if it were her first time on the telephone. Here's how her script read.

"Mr. Johnson? Mr. Johnson, my name is Delores Crenshaw from the University of California Alumni Association. We're, um, currently running a membership drive where we, um, uh, we'd like to find out if you would, um, like to participate in this, uh, membership drive."

At one point I interrupted her and said, "What do you want?" She didn't have an answer, since it wasn't on her script. My interruption caused her to start again at the very beginning: "Mr. Johnson, my name is Delores Crenshaw from the University of California Alumni Association." This poor woman was so bad with her script that the least variation caused her not only to forget it but to botch it. I felt for her, since she was probably struggling to pay her tuition.

Her problem was that she had not spent any time rehearsing and being comfortable with the script. How you come across verbally will determine whether you get an appointment with your prospect or make the sale. This does not mean you have to think off the top of your head. The best way even for experienced phone salespeople is to practice a script until you know it by heart.

You're probably wondering, "Won't it sound canned if I use a script?" No. It will only sound canned if you don't know it very well. Actors on TV shows follow a script even to the point of taking breaths at the right time. I once sat in an audience attending a sitcom for a popular TV show. While it was not a live audience taping, I was able to watch numerous takes and retakes solely because one of the actors had forgotten to use the word "the." Funny. They made him do a retake just because he got one word wrong.

If the actor is good, he doesn't seem to be reciting something from memory. He sounds spontaneous. This is exactly what must be done if you sell on the phone. If you know your script cold, you'll have the ability to vary from it when you need to. For example: if you're a new salesperson, one of the best ways to write a script is to get in contact with a top producer in your company. Simply record that top producer through four or five days of prospecting. Find out how they approach prospects, how they close, how they present, how they probe, and how they answer objections.

At this point, you can take the best part of the sales pitch, translate it, transcribe it, and then adapt it using your own words. Put it in written form, to generate your own script. Don't just listen to this person. Record them. If you simply listen, not only will you not hear the other side of the conversation, but you'll also forget much of what is said.

You need to have the written script in front of you as a resource. When Joy first started with my company, she frankly didn't know how we made money, let alone what to say to my prospects and clients. For about three weeks, I recorded my phone conversations. I then edited them for Joy to use. I gave her ten ways to approach prospects depending on their position in the company. I gave her eight questions to ask new prospects. I gave her twenty word-for-word presentations depending on the questions that were answered. I then gave her five closing techniques. I had another secretary type these sentences out and have them laminated. Simply knowing that she has this resource helped her feel better about making calls. She's never stuck, and she's able to be spontaneous even though reading from the script.

One of my presentations is entitled "How to Read Your Client's Mind." I've been doing this program for over thirty-five years and know it word for word. The trick is to make the audience think it's the first time I've ever given the presentation. If they think it's a canned program, they won't listen, but knowing the presentation so well allows me to be very spontaneous with an audience.

I can pick out certain members of the audience, bring participants up to the front, banter with them, and engage them. I can always go right back to my memorized speech any time I want. It allows me enormous flexibility. Using a script will give you an extremely strong selling tool.

After you have written your script, practice it out loud twenty times alone. Twenty is the magical number that will work for you. As a speaker, I know that if I can practice any presentation twenty times, I'll have it memorized. If you practice a line twenty times, you'll be much more articulate and spontaneous, even if you have to read it. After you practice it twenty times, try to role-play with a friend.

One manager in a very large insurance company has developed this into an art. Bob Gascon, in Southern California, has both new and more experienced agents role-play approaches, objections, presentations, and closes. He'll give an objection. For example, "I'm not interested. I don't want to speak to you."

The agents will then look at the objections list on their sheet and either recite from memory or read it as spontaneously as possible. He has each of these people role-play each script sentence at least ten times to make sure that it's totally in memory. This is a very wise investment of time, because each person who goes through this process becomes a big producer within just a few weeks.

Have you watched the old cop show *Miami Vice?* Remember Lieutenant Castillo? I read an article about this fine actor in an airline magazine. The story was written by a journalist who happened to be on *Miami Vice* as an extra. He, coincidentally, played a journalist interviewing one of the stars during an episode. In the airline article, he wrote, "He arrived at 7:00 a.m., three or four hours before filming was to start. No actors were on the set except for Lieutenant Castillo. Lieutenant Castillo sat in a chair, staring at one of the motorhomes used for a dressing room."

When the journalist asked the actor why he was staring, he said, "I'm laying my cables." Laying your cables? He explained, "In acting, you really only need to know three lines at a time, because the director will only shoot three or four lines before he sets for the next scene or the next camera shot," but Lieutenant Castillo decided early on that he wanted to prepare himself by making those three lines as natural as possible. Playing a very difficult part, he wanted to prepare himself to totally convince the audience of who he was.

Obviously it's important to know your product inside and out. But 95 percent of the people who sell on the telephone try to wing it. As you know, only 20 percent of salespeople ever make it in the long term. It's good to be spontaneous, but spontaneity comes from enormously high levels of preparation.

Five

Polishing Your Voice

Does your voice sound good on the phone? Is it high, low, robust, squeaky? More importantly, how does your voice sound to your prospect or client? Here are some easy tips to use on the telephone to make sure your voice comes across as effectively as possible.

Make sure you speak 20 percent louder on the telephone than you do face-to-face. Even with recent software advances, phones can still sound fuzzy. Don't assume that your prospect can hear you as effectively as face-to-face.

Number two, show more enthusiasm on the telephone than you would in person. On the telephone, it is easy to pick up how excited you are to talk to your prospect or client.

This can be overdone. You can be too enthusiastic and actually lose business. I once heard a sales trainer say that for every one person you lose by overenthusiasm, you lose nine by too little. This may be true. I recommend you try to be only slightly more enthusiastic than your prospect or client.

Have you noticed that overly enthusiastic people tend to turn you off? There may be too much of a mismatch between you and them. In fact, one consultant I see fairly often irritates me on the telephone. He sounds so excited and so enthusiastic that I don't like talking to him on the phone. He's too much unlike me. I think of myself as a very positive and enthusiastic person, but I don't want to talk to anyone on the telephone who is substantially more or less enthusiastic than I am. I don't want to talk to people who talk more quickly or slowly than I do; neither do I want to talk to people who have voice tones that are vastly higher or lower than mine. It's called *matching your prospect*. People buy from people who are like them. They avoid people who are dissimilar.

Should your voice be high or low? Should you command a robust, gravelly voice, or a higher one? The answer is yes to both. The trick is to perfectly match your prospect's vocal patterns. If her voice is high, increase your pitch. If his voice is low, lower your voice at the same time, but in any event, project from your diaphragm. It will help you become clearer, and you won't sound squeaky on the telephone.

Recently at a conference, I listened to a man from New York speak to a group from Charlotte, North Carolina. (In California, we tend to speak fairly quickly, around the same pace as New Yorkers, although not with the same accent.) After the New Yorker was done speaking, a female member of the audience asked me what I thought of him. I told her I liked him a lot. She said to me she thought he was too slick, too sharp, too smooth. He mismatched her by talking too quickly and with an accent that was too dissimilar from her North Carolina style.

The normal speech rate is approximately 150 words a minute. In New York, it's 300 words a minute. Some individuals argue that in the Southeast United States, it's about twenty words a minute. So if your voice is slow, and you're talking to someone from California, speed up. If your voice is fast, and you're talking to someone from Mississippi. slow down. Otherwise it can create distrust.

I had a prospect once from Chattanooga, Tennessee. This man was a regional manager for a very large company. I was sure that his speech rate was only twelve words per hour. I would ask him a question, and he would take at least ten to fifteen seconds to answer it. He would even spend ten seconds between words. Do you think that was tough? You bet it was. It was an incredible stretch for me to mirror him, yet I did business with him, largely because I tried to speak more like him without forcing him to speak like me.

Here's a tip that will help a prospect on the telephone buy from you a little more quickly. You've just learned to be similar to your prospect by matching their voice speed, pace, and pitch. But there's a large amount of research from the University of Michigan indicating that you can cause a prospect to buy more quickly from you by talking faster—up to a certain point.

How can you work this if you have a prospect that talks slowly? First, you simply match and mirror your prospect's voice, pace, rhythm, and vocal patterns. Then speed up after a few minutes. This is one of the most effective techniques you can use, especially in booking appointments or closing business.

I had a staff person once who was as good on the telephone as anybody I've ever heard. Not only was she able to book an enormous amount of business over the telephone, but she was asked to go on dates at least two or three times a week by people who didn't even live in California. This woman would first match and mirror her prospect's vocal patterns and speed of speaking, and then slowly speed up until her prospects doubled their own speech rate. At one point, as I listened to her, she was talking so quickly that I could barely make out what she was saying ten feet across the room, yet she was in high rapport with her prospect. He thought she was not only more convincing but also more exciting.

Our phone prospects and clients didn't know what she looked like. She was at least fifty pounds overweight. But I was never surprised when I heard a client say how good he thought she was on the telephone or how much they wanted to see her.

If you encounter a prospect or a client who is unenthusiastic, don't worry. You can create more enthusiasm by starting out at the same unenthusiastic voice speed as theirs. Later on, speed up to a more enthusiastic level.

Would you like to find out how good your voice is on the telephone? Here's a great tip. Record yourself and listen. You can make a call on a VoIP phone or Google Voice and just record. You will be surprised at how you sound. Besides recording information for scripts, you can also determine how good your voice sounds. As you play it back, listen not just to what you say, but to how closely you match your prospect's vocal characteristics. Are you using too much emotion or too little?

Something else that is effective is to count the number of uhs and um, um, ums you use when talking to your prospect. If you sound too halting, your prospect or client will think of you as unknowledgeable. You may also break rapport by hesitating too much.

From the recording, you also will hear an indication of your level of sincerity and comfort. You can bet your prospect knows your comfort level just by listening. The recording will let you know if your voice conveys sincerity, honesty, and urgency. These really are some of the most important reasons why your prospects buy from you.

Recently, a telephone salesperson got a phone call back from a prospect who didn't even want to do business with her. This salesperson told me that her prospect called back and said, "I don't want to buy anything from you and didn't really want to call you back, but you sounded so sincere when I talked to you on the phone last time that I did want to tell you why I'm not interested."

It is practically unheard of to have an uninterested prospect call you back. Although the salesperson didn't make the sale, she also found out why the prospect was not going to buy. Sometimes knowing why you *didn't* make a sale is better than knowing why you did. It helps you strengthen your weaknesses.

Another idea that will help you become more enthusiastic is to put a mirror in front of the telephone. It may seem obvious that if you smile while you're making phone calls, you will become more enthusiastic, but later that smile will dissipate. A mirror lets you know that you have to smile; it will also let you know when you don't. It'll tell you when you're enthusiastic and when you're not.

Six

Perfecting the Art of Listening

I spent many years evaluating and researching why some salespeople make money over the phone and why others are not as effective. I have noticed that the extremely high-profit salespeople make more because of the way they listen. These big hitters have told me that they are so profitable because they listen better than anybody else.

I've also noticed over the years that most sales are not lost because of bad closing techniques, but because the salesperson missed an objection. They were lost because of poor listening.

I evaluated one salesperson who had problems because he already knew what the prospect wanted. This is especially bad on the telephone, because no matter how much you think you know about your prospects' and clients' business, they want to feel unique. They want to be recognized as having concerns and problems that are different from anyone else's. Even if you've heard this story a dozen times this week, prospects want to know that you'll help them solve their own unique problems.

One way to become a better listener is to ask a question within the first fifteen seconds and then let the prospect talk. Remember that I talked about how to contact referrals? I also mentioned how to get rapport after you've introduced yourself and stated your purpose. Asking questions in the first fifteen seconds makes that effective. If you ask a question within the first fifteen seconds, you'll get the prospect involved and establish in their mind that you care and want to solve their problems.

For example, "I understand you run the marketing department. What exactly do you do?" Or "Tom tells me that you travel a lot visiting your regions. How many offices do you have?" Asking a question immediately not only diverts your prospect's attention from the fact that you've interrupted him, but also establishes in their mind that you're concerned.

Have you ever noticed what really takes place when people buy? In various research studies as well as from my own personal experience in evaluating top salespeople, I've found that prospects rarely ever buy because of what you say. *They buy because of what they say to themselves.* If you're able to change your prospect's attitude toward your product, it's because he's convinced himself rather than because you convinced him.

Knowing this, doesn't it now make more sense that you can never talk someone into buying? You have to *listen* them into buying. The prospect must convince himself. He will never convince himself if you're doing all the talking.

I recently spoke at a conference in Oakland, California. One of the sponsors was a real-estate executive. I was trying to get him to use me to speak at some of his sales meetings. One of his associates spoke to him about me. I followed up on the phone after the conference and said, "Dick, I want to talk to you about doing regional sales conferences. I'd like to ask you more questions about what your salespeople need." He immediately gave me an objection. He said, "Well, I don't know that I think our salespeople really need your kind of presentations. I think they need more product information about loans and financing techniques."

It was difficult, but I bit my tongue and didn't jump in, even though I really wanted to fight that objection and set the guy straight. Instead I listened. I just said, "Well, I understand." Then he hesitated for about five seconds. I'm glad I didn't interrupt. I just listened, because soon he reversed himself.

"Then again," he said, "we've had enough product information to last a long time. I've had a few of our associates say to me recently they would like more sales-based, people-skills training. I guess, Kerry, your kind of presentation is very timely. Why don't we do this? Why don't you speak at our conference next month on the fourteenth?"

If I had interrupted him by overcoming his objection as soon as I heard it, I would have talked myself right out of a sale. But I simply listened and let him state what he thought in entirety, so I let him talk himself into a sale rather than having me talk him out of it.

In short, when you're new in selling on the telephone, you try to talk people into buying. When you're more experienced, you listen for openings, and then try to talk them into buying. But when you're a peak performer, a top producer, you listen your prospect into buying. This means that your prospect came up with their own conclusions, prompted by you. She'll buy her own ideas long before she buys yours.

How to Become a Great Listener

Here are some tips that will help you become a better listener on the telephone.

1. Listen accurately. Psychologists have known for years that a key tool in their treasure chest of counseling techniques is to rephrase their clients' comments. This is often difficult but extremely effective. For example, the client says, "Well, I'm having some problems with cash flow in my company." Your response might be something like, "Cash-flow difficulties, huh?" Or "Money difficulties, is that it?"

   He might say, "I want to decrease my taxes. I think I'm paying too much." Your response might be, "Too much to the government, huh?" If you can rephrase his comments in your own words, you can also create more rapport. They will give you more information.

2. Reject the prospect; don't let them reject you. In other words, do three times as much listening as you do talking. As you probe, make sure you retain the option of disqualifying them. If you do all the talking, they will reject or disqualify you. If you think you can help, then during the presentation stage, keep your solutions focused on what you can do to solve his problems.

3. Listen affirmatively, not negatively. As your prospect talks, say things like, "Yes, got it. Interesting! Right!" This will reassure your prospect that you appreciate their comments and are empathetic. When they hear these kinds of words, they will be

more open to talking to you. This may work so well that your problem might be that your prospect talks too much to you.

4. Every so often, summarize what you've heard so far. More sales have been spoiled by not getting your prospect to agree on the issues. Too many salespeople assume that what they heard is what the prospect said. It's not what you *heard* that's important, it's what your prospect *meant*.

At a conference recently, I spoke about the behaviors of very top salespeople. I said that the best had sales commissions of $1.3 million per year and up. One attendee came up to me after my presentation and said, "Gee, I do three times that amount of production."

"Really?" I said. "How much?" He thought that production meant *volume* of sales. I meant production as in *commissions* from sales. When he found out that I meant commissions, he was shocked that anyone could make that much.

It doesn't matter who miscommunicated. The only thing that mattered was that he perceived something different than what I said. As for understanding my speech, I missed the boat. It was my mistake, not his, but your telephone prospect may not take responsibility so readily.

Here's a listening exercise to find out quickly how good you are at paying attention. Are you ready for this test?

You're the bus driver. The bus goes south 4.4 miles, east 3.3 miles, north 2.2 miles, and then back 1.1 mile. Based on the information, how old is the bus driver? What do you think?

There's no set answer. The bus driver is your age, since I said *you* are the bus driver. The age of the bus driver is how old you are right now. Did you pay attention?

The Importance of Probing

If you want to close more effectively, you first must know how to listen or probe. I can't overestimate the importance of probing well. If your prospect doesn't think you know exactly what he wants and what he needs, he may and will reject your solution. The degree and amount of rejection you receive depends on how well you probe. If you probe extremely well, that is, you find out exactly what your prospect wants and needs and how he will buy, you will receive very few objections. If you don't probe at all, his objections may be so intense that you will not be able to close. In other words, if you present your product ideas without first probing and determining your prospect's needs, you will get far more objections.

Have you ever heard the adage that if you want to make a sale, find a need and fill it? Well, finding a need is much easier than creating one. People who present and talk their prospect into buying are basically *creating* a need. People who probe are *finding* a need. You'll sell two or three times as much by finding their needs than trying to create them.

A telephone salesperson recently called me trying to sell fine art. I didn't think I needed to buy art. He asked me about my office and the decorations. I don't think I even found out his name, but he sure knew a lot about me. He probed so well in asking about my office decor that after the conversation I sincerely felt that I needed some of his artwork. He never even mentioned how much it cost, but I found myself wanting to own it. This is a good example of something I didn't think I needed, yet by probing effectively, he found a need.

I do a presentation on the topic "Sales Magic: How to Double Production." At the end of the program, I try to get the attendees to practice what they've just heard by selling pens to one another. I was astounded at what I found during the first six months of doing this. In almost every case, when I said to sell a pen to your neighbor, the attendees would take a pen out their pocket, look at it, and say, "Isn't this a nice pen? Isn't this a pretty gold color? Would you like to buy it? It's only $10."

Only 10 to 15 percent of the time did they ask their partner what kind of pen they liked or what style was most important to them. Did they like gold or black? Did they like black or blue ink? Did they like fat or thin pens? Rarely did somebody probe, asking the right questions.

Even now, when I speak on this topic, I ask, "How many of you bought the pen?" Rarely do more than 20 percent ever raise their hands.

The most important part of the sales process is something you are probably not doing enough of. Probing is so important that I pick my staff depending on how well they probe me during the interview process. I'm not as concerned what the level of experience my interviewees have. I'm not as concerned about their skill set. I am concerned about how they probe and ask questions. I'm trying to sell them on working for me. They're trying to sell me on hiring them. In my consulting business, I have found that if I interview a potential employee who simply answers questions and tells me how great they are, they rarely succeed with my company, but with those individuals who ask me questions and probe to determine the strategy I will use in hiring, the chances of their working out and being successful are considerable.

Once you have probed from a referral lead or even a cold call, immediately go into questions to try to uncover the product benefits that will help most. Before you talk or say anything about your product, first find out their needs or problems, which will aid you in presenting your product's benefits.

One successful salesperson once told me that he never asked a prospect a question that he doesn't know the answer to. While this probably works for him, generally it's an idiotic strategy. Probing is used to determine how your prospect will buy and what is important to him. If you ask a question you already know the answer to, you're actually saying that you are too limited in what you present.

The sharper salespeople have an enormous number of options to prescribe depending on what their client needs. A physician doesn't ask you a question about your illness already knowing what you're going to say. He asks you questions about your symptoms to determine how to diagnose your problem. Be a physician with your prospects. Be a doctor in determining how to solve their problems and reach solutions.

If you're trying to sell a product like a pen to your prospect over the telephone, ask questions like, "Do you erase your writing very often?" "Do you like pens that conform to your hand?" "Do you like thin or fat pens, or any particular style of pen?" "When using mechanical pencils, Mr. Jones, where do you like to clip them—on the top, the bottom? Where is it most comfortable?" This is just good, plain, basic fact finding.

Here's a rule: never present your ideas without first finding what your prospect wants—even if your prospect asks specific questions about your product.

I found this out the hard way. I called a prospect on the telephone a couple of years ago—a strong referral. This regional manager immediately asked how much I charged to do a program. I first wanted to find out how big his group was, how long he wanted me to speak, whether it was a weekend program, and the topic they needed most. Instead I let him intimidate me into telling him how much I charged.

As soon as I told him my fee, he said, "Oh, that's too much. We can't afford you. I'm busy, have to go. Bye-bye." He blew me off the telephone. I'd let him force me into presenting before I was ready. Prescription without diagnosis is malpractice. I learned my lesson.

A short time later, I made a referral phone call to a Prudential-Bache brokerage manager in the San Francisco area. Again, a strong referral. I called and said, "I recently spoke to a Pru-Bache top-producer meeting in Hawaii. One of the reps in attendance, Darlene Hamilton, referred me to you, thinking you may need a speaker like me at your next conference."

"How much do you charge?" he said.

"Well, it's difficult for me to say," I said. "I'd first like to find out the number of people at the program and what they need most to learn, as well as other information."

He tried to be intimidating. He said, "I don't want you to waste my time. I want to know how much you charge."

I said, "If I told you how much I charged, it would be either too high or too low, and frankly, sir, I don't know until I find out more about your company."

This gentleman said to me, "If you don't tell me how much you charge, I'm not going to waste my time on the telephone with you."

Refusing to be intimated this time, I said, "I understand that you don't want to waste your time on the telephone. If I told you what my fees were right now, it would waste your time and also mine."

He laughed on the telephone and said, "What would you like to know?"

I called his bluff. If I had acquiesced, he would have blown me off the telephone. If I had told him my fee without attaching value to it first, he would not have bought my services.

You should be asking how to make a smooth transition from approaching a prospect to probing on the phone. If you make that transition smoothly, you'll turn fairly high rapport into information you can use to make a sale. If the prospect is rough, he may give you an objection and try to blow you off the telephone as well.

The smoother you make that transition, the more trust the prospect will have in you. The more trust he puts in you, the less time it will take you to sell, and the higher your closing rate will be.

Two things you need to know in making a smooth bridge from approach to probe is using the word *you* as often as possible. This not only keeps the prospect focused on the telephone call, but helps him to realize that you are trying to help him personally. Also, make sure that you give that prospect a quick benefit to justify and substantiate why you want to take his time to ask him questions.

Here's an example. "Mr. Thomas, we've been able to increase sales for several companies like yours over the last three years using our IT systems. While I'm not sure our systems are appropriate for you, I would like to ask you a couple of questions to determine whether it will be a contribution to you."

Now not only is he ecstatic that you're interested in helping his sales, but more importantly, he knows you are not trying to sell him something without first finding out what his individual needs are.

The Takeaway

Let's face it: sometimes you'll receive an objection before you get a chance to probe. Sometimes a prospect may try to blow you off the phone by saying, "You can't help me. I'm not interested. We already have someone who can handle what you're trying to sell. I'm afraid you're wasting my time." Any one of these objections in the first few minutes can be handled very well with the takeaway type of bridging into a probe.

The trick is to avoid eliciting objections from your prospect before you probe. The takeaway basically promises an incredible benefit, but you stop short of claiming the prospect will get it unless he fulfills certain criteria. Here's how it works.

"Mr. Thomas, I'm not sure this service can help you, but I'd like to ask you a couple of questions. My clients have increased their sales by 35 percent with our products. That may not happen with your company, but I'd like to ask you a couple of quick questions to find out."

You can imagine what your prospect is thinking. You make a comment like that, he's on the spot thinking, "Why couldn't I get that kind of a benefit? What's wrong with my company that we wouldn't be able to increase our sales by that much? We're just as good as anybody else. We can save money using your services like anybody else can." The takeaway frequently works, but it must be kept subtle.

I once prospected a manager with the old EF Hutton securities corporation. The manager was a little bit negative when I introduced myself, so I decided to use a fairly crafty technique with him. After introducing myself and gaining a little bit of rapport from my referral, I said to him, "Bob, I recently did a presentation for a Prudential-Bache regional broker conference. The regional director said that sales increased by 71 percent for three months after I spoke there. Now this may not happen with EF Hutton, but I sure would like to ask some questions to see if I may be a contribution to your brokers."

This manager on the spot said, "Well, you know, our brokers are much sharper than Prudential-Bache's. I'm sure we can get a bigger increase in sales than them." He was actually selling himself because of the takeaway.

There is a pitfall in using this technique. It's important to avoid being condescending. Your style here is as important as what you say. It's important to allow the prospect to prove to you why he's a better candidate than the other clients you've had.

Would you like to know why this works? It's very simple. Your prospect is very used to being hyped on the telephone by people claiming the moon. When he hears somebody also claiming high benefits but making him qualify for them, all of a sudden he moves in to try to prove you he is just as good as everybody else.

In all the years that I've been using the takeaway technique, I've never had a prospect say, "Well, I bet we can't get the same benefits as your other clients. I bet our production won't increase as much as others." They're trying to prove themselves more qualified, not less.

Here are some examples of the bridge-to-probe and takeaway techniques.

KERRY: John, I'm able to help my clients not only save money but also buy rental property at a reasonable price. I'd like to ask you a few questions about whether I might be able to help you.

JOHN: Some questions?

KERRY: Yes, this won't take long.

JOHN: OK.

KERRY: Ms. Smith, my name is Kerry Johnson with Lost Capital Leasing. Hi.

NANCY: Hi.

KERRY: We're a commercial leasing company here in Southern California. I've been able to help numerous companies like yours acquire affordable office space. I realize this might not be right for you, but I would like to ask you a couple of questions to determine whether I will be able to make a contribution when you next decide to move your business to a new building.

NANCY: OK.

Seven
How to Qualify a Prospect

Have you ever done a great job of finding your prospect's needs, but as you closed, you discovered they really weren't the decision maker? He may have said to you, "Well, I'd love to buy this, but I'm not the guy to sell." Or "I don't make those kinds of decisions, but I know who does."

It would be nice if everybody told you exactly who the decision maker was and never led you on. Unfortunately, many prospects you'll come in contact with love to assume power, especially if they don't have any in the first place.

Unfortunately for you, you can't waste time talking to everybody in the company. You need to quickly find the right person, the one who has the authority and power to buy. It's important to find out who the decision maker is up front before you present your product; otherwise you may be sabotaged.

Two things will happen if you present to the wrong person. Number one, you may give him too much information, so he arbitrarily says no to you even though he's not even the person who can say yes. In other words, he can block access to the decision maker.

Number two, you may give him so much information that you can't go over his head. He may force you to go only through him. Craig, a friend of mine in Lansing, Michigan, is a top insurance producer. He's so good, in fact, that he's made the Million Dollar Round Table every year for the last ten years. He recently he told me about a phone call to a prospect who was the VP of finance.

He assumed that this guy was the decision maker. It was an easy mistake, because the vice president acted like the decision maker, asking the agent specific questions to find out if the product was appropriate. My friend booked an appointment and met him face-to-face. Eventually he got to the close and said, "Well, what do you think?"

The vice president said, "Looks great to me, but I have to pass this by the president for approval." Craig immediately realized that he had spent two weeks with the wrong guy. He should have gone to the president instead, without wasting time with someone who couldn't say yes. Don't sell someone who can't buy.

Having worked with the wrong person, now he couldn't simply bypass the vice president and go directly to the president. He had to sell all over again to the president, but if the vice president felt alienated, he may have tried to sabotage the sale. Or the VP could have presented the product himself, again ensuring a no. This is even worse. Do you think someone else can sell your product better than you? In effect, the agent left an important sale to someone who didn't know anything about it.

Here's a quick question that you may like to ask a prospect from now on to determine if he really is the decision maker. Say, "Mr. Jones, who else is involved in this decision besides you?" He'll say,

"No one. It's my decision." Or he'll say, "Well, I guess Mr. Thomas will have to be in on it."

"Oh, who's he?"

"He's the director of marketing. He cuts all the checks." By probing the relationship between Mr. Jones and Mr. Thomas a little bit more closely, you will have determined whom you should be talking to. If you have made contact with the wrong person, you can at least use that prospect as a springboard to get to the decision maker. Don't alienate your prospect by hurting his ego. Say something like this: "Would you mind if I had a chat with Mr. Thomas?"

You could then go to the right decision maker and say, "Mr. Jones thought that you might be the right person to talk to. My name is Kerry Johnson, and I'd like to talk to you about increasing your sales with our IT systems." Asking, "Who else will decide on this besides you?" will get great information on who the decision maker really is. It's a good technique for avoiding rejection during the closing stage when you find out you're talking to the wrong person.

Sometimes even the right decision maker will stall you or try get more time. He'll claim that he has to run it by some other people. Make sure that you get your prospect on the phone to admit up front that he is the decision maker. Get him to admit during the probe, when rapport is high. You won't get an objection later on.

For example, if he says, "Gee, I really have to run this by my vice president," your response would be, "I thought that during our initial phone call, you said that you were the guy who made the final decision." He has no place to go. He can't say he was lying. He admitted it in the first place. You've saved yourself valuable money and time.

Remember, if you don't get to the decision maker and let somebody else sell for you, your closing rate will drop like a rock.

How to Deal with Committees

Committees have to be the worst institution that man has ever created. Even Peter Drucker, the great management expert, once said, "A committee is an anarchy held together by a parking lot." If someone tells you it's a decision to be made by a group of people, save yourself headache and forget about it.

You'll often hear prospects say, "Well, it's a committee decision. It's really up to the committee members. I'll present it to the committee and see what they decide." There will always be a person on that committee who will sabotage you.

Make sure that you find out who heads the committee. Ask your prospect, "Who really runs the committee?" He may say, "Well, I guess I do." Or he may make it tougher on you: "Nobody runs the committee. We all have a voice in the decisions."

That's sincere garbage. When was the last time you heard about a company or any association of people who all had equal power? It simply doesn't happen. Obviously there are differences among people. There are always those who are going to be more aggressive than others. There's always someone who is in a greater position of leadership than anybody else.

If you get stalled like this, I recommend you say, "I understand that this is a group decision, but who is really the strongest voice on the committee?"

"I guess that's Jim Thompson."

"Would you mind if I chatted with him?"

"No, I don't mind at all. Would you like his phone number?"

Make sure that you always get the name of the person heading the committee. If you get to the strong person and sell him, you will in effect get the rest of the committee members to rubber-stamp your idea. If you do not get the head of the committee, your sale will be about as easy as picking fly poop out of pudding with a boxing glove.

What if you're not dealing with businesses that have presidents or owners who can make decisions? What if you're a stockbroker trying to solicit business from a family? Certainly you'll ask who the decision maker really is here, but the male might be insulted that you even asked.

Here's a tip to use in this kind of situation: make sure that you find out who the decision maker is among the husband and wife, but be crafty and clever as you ask. Use these words: "You make your own decisions, don't you?"

If he doesn't, he will tell you, "Well, my wife and I talk about things like this together."

Guess what. You better get both of them together when you sell. It's very likely she will have an impact on his decision. On the other hand, she may be a very valued resource for his decisions or vice versa. All the more reason to get them together when you talk to them about, for example, insurance or investments.

I need to be candid with you right now. I've had salespeople call me and ask me to buy insurance, stocks, mutual funds, bonds, even awnings for my house. At the time they close, I hate to admit it, but I almost always say, "Well, it's really my wife's decision. She the one who makes decisions on things like this."

Whether she does or not, I usually stall everyone. But if you ask at the very beginning, "Do you make your own decisions?" you will prevent me, among your other prospects, from stalling you. Get your prospect to admit whether or not he is the decision maker during the probing phase.

Sorting out the Chaff

Are you good at qualifying? Do you find out quickly in probing interviews whether or not your prospect is a good candidate for your product or service? Just as importantly, do you find out quickly whether your prospect can afford your product? During the probing interview, you need to have the ability to make sure the prospect can not only afford your product, but has a need for it.

Most good stockbrokers early on dial the telephone at least forty to fifty times per hour and make sometimes as many as 150 to 200 calls per day. The really good ones spend no more than four to five minutes on a phone call and only talk more than thirty seconds if the prospect shows some degree of initial interest.

Sophisticated and sharp telephone salespeople find out quickly whether their prospect is a real, qualified cherry or a cherry-coated pit. They use what's called a *trial close* bridged in the qualification. Here's the way some stockbrokers qualify. After they have talked about the stock market and after they have mentioned mutual funds and how great market conditions are, they simply say, "Mr. Jones, if I found an investment idea that could get you 10 percent more per year, would you have any trouble investing $20,000 right now?"

Sure, there's always the chance that the prospect would lie, but barring that difficulty, if the prospect says, "I really don't have that kind of money lying around," then get off the telephone. If he says, "Sure, if it's a good investment and I can accomplish my goals. I could get the money together quickly." Now you have a qualified prospect.

It's important to qualify for money after you present some kind of benefit. In other words, don't qualify for money too early. You may scare your prospect, but after they receive some value or an idea of how your product will benefit them, a qualification for money is very appropriate.

Remember, don't present the cost of your product before the value is established, but there's nothing stopping you from asking a qualification question early on.

In my business, we often ask a prospect in the first two or three minutes how many people will be at a meeting. If there's under 100, I will rarely negotiate my speaking fee, but if there's over 100 people, I'm very motivated to negotiate my fee. If there's under twenty people, I don't want to do the program at all.

We spend a lot of time tracking down the perfect, qualified prospect for my business. We know how many people work for her. We know what her budget is. We know what her needs are. We know how motivated she is. When I find a prospect, I try to make sure that her business and psychological makeup are as close to the perfect prospect as I can get. That's how we qualify.

Another way to qualify is the survey approach. This is especially effective in making cold calls. Since it's important to gain your prospect's attention in the first thirty seconds, asking survey questions will not only grab him, but will also give him something he'll enjoy doing.

People love answering survey questions. They love to be part of a survey that may be published someplace. When I was at Walt Disney World in Orlando, Florida, I went on an attraction that was basically a glorified survey. All the hostesses did was instruct us to sit on the chairs with a button in the arm, letting us look at television commercials. The line to get into the attraction was wrapped around the building.

Here's an example of a survey question used to qualify: "Mr. Franks, I'm from TDY Communications. I'm not sure our Internet

5G service can help you, but I would like to ask you a couple of questions to find out. How fast is your Internet connection right now? How much is your overall monthly bill? How many people share the bandwidth you have? How important is video to your business?"

If the prospect is a sole proprietor, he may not warrant discount rates. If the monthly telephone bill is under, say, $100, he may not be a good prospect to deal with. He may take too much of your time.

Qualifying well will make sure you spend 80 percent of your time on the 20 percent, or the most productive prospects. Without qualifying effectively, you'll earn 20 percent of your dollars from 80 percent of your prospects, thereby wasting your time.

Eight
Probing

Do you always know on the phone how your prospect will decide to buy? When you book an appointment from a phone conversation, do you find out quickly how he will decide to give you an appointment? When you do see him face-to-face, do you learn how he will decide to buy your product?

You can determine this very quickly if you ask the right questions. If you don't find out your prospect's decision strategy ahead of time, you'll never reach a100 percent closing rate. If you ask the right questions, your prospect will literally let you know ahead of time how they will buy. When you do present your product or service, you will know exactly what they will be most interested in. Using this information the right way will precipitate your prospect's decision to purchase.

Using a Wedge

Let's take a few situations. Does your prospect already have a vendor? If you're an insurance agent, does he already have another insurance agent? If you're a broker, does he already have another somewhere else? Is your prospect already using consultants? Will you have to compete against someone else he's currently using?

One rule, which you already know, is that you shouldn't knock other competitors. There's a very good reason behind this. Not only is it tacky to cut someone down behind their back, but chances are if you cut a competitor in front of your prospect, they will defend the vendor whether they like him or not.

Realizing that, you can find out a lot about your prospect's relationship with the vendor by using phrases like this. "You use GBS business services. I've heard that they're a good company. What do you really like about GBS?"

Your prospect will say, "Well, the counselor is truthful. He's a good negotiator. He works very hard for me." You say, "Sounds like you're very pleased with him." Here you're actually supporting the competitor rather than knocking him. You're actually building him up to the point that your prospect may tell you on the spot what he doesn't like about that vendor.

For example, I was in the midst of trying to secure a consulting contract with a very large construction firm. When I called my prospect from a referral call, I asked some probing questions in an effort to find out his relationship with one of my competitors, which the company was already utilizing. He said, "We're already using Dan Thompson for sales training."

"Tony," I said, "I've heard great things about Dan Thompson. What do you like about him?"

"Well, he has good delivery. My salespeople seem to like him. He's on target with what my guys do day in and day out."

I then said, "It sounds like he's doing a super job for you."

At that point, my prospect backed down a little bit and started to get honest. I was, in effect, building the competition up too much in my prospect's eyes. So he found a few faults. He said, "Well, Dan's good, but I would like to see more out of him. He does basically one approach, and that's a fairly manipulative closing program. I think my salespeople have to do too much to apply his techniques to their business."

Aha. I found a chink in the armor. I found out what my prospect dislikes about my competition without cutting my competition down.

Of course, you could use phrases like, "Are you getting what you want from your vendor right now?" This may work, but again your prospect may see this as a slam against your competition and, unfortunately, defend them.

Another great line is to flat out ask your prospect what perfection is in his words. This is extremely effective in making introductory phone calls and probing for information. You might say something like, "Let's assume you really had a perfect experience in buying a house. What does a perfect realtor mean to you?" This is a very effective and informative question. The prospect undoubtedly has an idea of what he wants. (I promise your competition won't ask questions like this.)

Your prospect may answer, "A perfect realtor is someone who gets me a great investment house at a great price." This gives you a lot of information on what the prospect wants. He doesn't want a pool. He wants a great investment. He doesn't want schools nearby. He wants a great price.

Your next question might be, "Are you getting that right now from your existing realtor?" You see, you can really find out how people will buy if you ask them very simple questions. More importantly, you can create a wedge between them and their vendor by getting them to tell you what they would like to improve. Then present a solution based on what they want but aren't getting.

Can People Change?

Let me ask you another question. Do you believe that people really can change anytime they want if there's enough need, motivation, and desire?

If you answered no, people really don't change substantially, you're absolutely right. There are two ways to change, number one, by religious conversion, and number two, by brain surgery. Everything else is only very slight modification.

Let me prove it to you. Have you ever tried to stop smoking? You're probably thinking, "Yes, Kerry. Of course, I have. I stopped seventeen times." In the context of all the behaviors that make up who you are, smoking is very small. There's a lot more to you than that, yet changing your smoking habit is an extremely difficult thing to do.

Do you have friends who are divorced? Do they have perfect marriages the second time around? Chances are, they have equally bad or equally good marriages the second time, largely because the spouse changed, but your friend didn't. They thought the problem was the spouse from the marriage before. But the problem was with them and the way they behaved, both before and now.

Jean Piaget, father of much of current psychological thought, discovered that over 90 percent of the makeup you have in your personality was developed between the ages of two and seven years old. Even making very slight modifications afterward is often traumatic.

Now that we know this, does it also make sense that if people don't change their personality characteristics very quickly, they may also have great difficulty changing their buying habits? And that the way your prospect bought before is very likely the way they will buy in the future?

Instant Replay

You're about to learn a technique that is simple, but is one of the most powerful concepts you can ever use on the phone. It's called *instant replay*. It's based on getting your prospect's past buying behavior. Here's a real-estate example.

"Mr. James, how did you decide to buy that house over on Elm Street?"

He might say, "It had a great pool in the backyard and a gorgeous view. It was on a quiet street."

It doesn't matter what he tells you is on his wish list for the next house. The strategy he will use and the benefits he will care about most in his next house are exactly the things he thought were important in his last house. People just don't change.

While you're probing on the telephone, write down how they bought before. When you get to the presentation stage, you know exactly what to do. Present exactly those benefits that you thought were the reasons he made his last purchase.

The "Let's Assume" Technique

Another technique is future planning. or the "let's assume" technique. Have you ever had a prospect who has never bought a product like yours? Try to put this prospect into the future. Say this.

"Mr. James, you want a new house with more room. I want you to imagine for a moment that we are done with the mortgage process. What happened that let you know it was a great experience, and you and I had a great relationship?"

What is he going to say? "I got the loan. The adjustable mortgage didn't go up by 50 percent. The neighborhood is quiet." He will say that the broker kept in contact every two days. There were no surprises at the closing, and the broker helped him work through any issues. Guess how he'll decide to buy that house. If you're sharp, you'll give him assurances that the mortgage will not increase substantially. You'll assure him that you will call every two days, and there will be no surprises at the closing.

If you do these things, you will find out how that prospect will make a decision, and if you present to those three needs, you will make a sale. Here's an example of getting your prospect's buying strategy.

KERRY: Gordon, out of curiosity, have you ever bought health insurance before?

GORDON: Yes, a couple of years ago.

KERRY: How did you decide to buy the plan back then?

GORDON: Well, it only cost about $375 per employee back then, but the biggest reason was that they were fully covered except for the $500 deductible.

KERRY: Which is more important, the coverage or the $375 premiums?

GORDON: Oh, for sure, the coverage.

After you have determined what your prospect thinks and what her most important needs are, try to confirm and prioritize what she said later. It's called *confirming the criteria* that she will use to make a decision. What you are really doing is reestablishing the criteria of the decision strategy. For example: "According to what you mentioned, price seems to be the most important thing, correct?" Or "According to what you've mentioned on time delivery, it seems to me the most important thing to you right now. Is that right?"

This sorts out your prospect's concerns. Play those concerns back, and let them prioritize the most important things. This relates well to your prospect's buying strategy, which we talked about before. But this also gives your prospect time, after he's given you information, to tell you what the most and least important things are. He will actually prioritize them for you.

At the end, it's very important to say, "Is there anything else I need to know to correctly understand your needs? Is there anything else you would like to tell me to give me more information on solving some of your concerns and problems?"

Your prospect has a worry list. If you take items off his worry list, he's more likely to buy from you, and the more trust and rapport he has, the more he'll tell you. The more he tells you, the better your chance to take items of his worry list.

Closed and Open-Ended Questions

Probably a salesperson's best tool on the phone is to know how to use closed and open-ended questions. Closed-end questions are those that give you a yes and no answer. Open-ended questions allow your prospect to give you more information than just yes or no. The technique that hard-closing salespeople use over the telephone is to constantly ask closed-end questions. You can just imagine that it's part of their script where they ask a question that have yes and no inside the sentence.

For example, when I was contacted by my college's alumni association, the ineffective salesperson said, "You would like to support your alma mater, wouldn't you?" She was basically asking for a yes or no. "Did you enjoy your college experience?" Again expecting a yes or no answer. She even phrased it in such a way as to get me to only say yes, so I would donate money.

A much better way to generate rapport is to let your prospect do most of the talking. Your prospect can't say more than yes or no unless you ask open-ended questions. This is a fairly easy concept to understand, yet many salespeople miss the point by not using open-ended questions effectively.

Don't elicit a yes or no answer. Granted, closed-end questions are effective if you want to get off the telephone quickly, but they're not effective for developing rapport between you and the prospect. Using open-ended questions will help you get enough information to make that sale.

I sometimes use closed-ended questions to get specific information that I don't want the prospect to talk about. For example, when I ask his address I say, "Are you at 2012 Mulberry Avenue?"

"Yes."

"How long have you lived there?"

"Ten years."

An open-ended question might be, "How did you decide on moving to Mulberry Avenue?" Or "Tell me about your past experience with other IT salespeople." These questions will yield vast amounts of information about how your prospect will make decisions and what he likes and dislikes, as well as about his needs. As you can see, open-ended questions elicit much more trust by getting your prospect to give information along with his answer.

A CPA once gave me an illustration of an improper use of closed-ended questions that yield very little information. Some gentleman in a hot-air balloon saw two men in a field below and yelled down, "Hey, down there. Where are we?" One of the men looked up and said, "You are there."

One man in the balloon said, "It must have been a CPA who answered the question."

His friend said, "How did you know that?"

"He answered my question perfectly, but gave me very little information I could use."

This is very much like the kind of information you will get from closed-ended questions if used improperly. You'll get exactly what you asked for, but little about how that prospect thinks.

This relates very well to meeting the opposite sex. When I was single, I listened to how guys would try to pick up women. Many single men used to make big mistakes in approaching women. They would go into a bar and ask questions like, "Do you come here often?" If you were a female, what would your response be, open or closed-ended? Obviously, closed. She would say no or yes. Most of the time, no.

If this question is trying to generate rapport and conversation, it misses the mark. It just doesn't work. Instead, if you're single and you want to meet somebody, try this. Walk into a bar and ask the girl this question: "What do you think of this bar?" Or "What do you think of the dancing here?"

It seems that good phone salespeople may have a better dating life once they learn some of the more advanced sales techniques.

Survey Selling

If you are using the telephone to book appointments, you can use a valuable probing technique. When you're using a survey to book an appointment, ask questions directly after your approach as part of the probe to get the appointment. Give a reason why you're asking the questions before you actually pose them.

One of the great benefits of using a survey is that you're actually getting information over the telephone ahead of time with your questions rather than just asking for an appointment. You're proving to your prospect through the probing process that you can help, rather than asking your prospect to trust you until they see you face-to-face.

Here's an example. "Mr. Prospect, my name is Kerry Johnson with Break Easy Health Insurance. I'd like to ask a couple of questions to determine whether I can be of service to you. We sometimes can save clients up to 30 percent on employee health premiums. How many employees do you have? What kind of coverage do you have? How much are your monthly premiums?"

At this point you would close your prospect on an appointment by saying, "Well, it sounds like I can save you some money. I'd like to see you to discuss these savings. Is Thursday at 2:00 or Friday at 4:00 better for you?" This is a very deductive process in which you have already gained rapport over the telephone, because your prospect has allowed you to ask questions initially. More importantly, by virtue of the information you found, you gave a benefit to the prospect: "It sounds like I may be able to save you some money."

At this point you posed a closing alternative-choice question regarding which day is best for a meeting. You won't often get an objection if you're as smooth as this going from a probe to a close. See if you can spot the closed-ended and open-ended questions in this survey approach.

KERRY: Sandy, I'd like to ask you a couple of questions to see if our personnel service can help you find good people more easily, OK?

SANDY: How long will this take?

KERRY: Oh, just a few minutes

SANDY: All right.

KERRY: How many employees do you have right now?

SANDY: Ten.

KERRY: What are the salary ranges?

SANDY: It's $25,000 to $50,000 a year.

KERRY: How do you find good people now?

SANDY: Usually through the Internet, but also by word of mouth.

KERRY: Is your attrition level acceptable currently?

SANDY: Oh, attrition is never acceptable. I would like to keep good people longer. We usually keep good people about a year.

KERRY: Well, I think I may be able to both save you money and find you quality people more quickly. Can you see me Monday in the afternoon at 3:45, or is 4:45 better?

SANDY: Oh, 4:45 would be better.

KERRY: Good. I know you'll find our meeting very productive.

Getting Past Looky Loos

Whether you're selling bicycles, insurance, stocks, bonds, or thumbtacks, you're likely to have a looky loo on the telephone sometimes. These people want to compare prices, services, and product benefits on the telephone before making a decision. The problem is, you aren't paid to explain and evaluate. You're paid to close.

These people often ask question after question, while their only purpose is to gather information. How much is it? Can you deliver it today? Can I get quantity discounts? How much is postage and handling? Will you throw in anything special? These are the types of questions that prospects ask just to get information. They're basically asking for free information even though they have absolutely no intention of buying from you.

The key to dealing with people who pump you for information is, don't get pumped unless you first get commitment. The way to get commitment is to close while answering questions. If your prospect asks a question, make sure that you answer it by also posing a closing question. Do this before you actually answer.

For example, his question might be, "Well, do you also offer annuities?" Your question is, "Are annuities what you're most interested in?"

"Will you give a 10 percent discount?"

Here's where the real closing skill comes in, but you must use it at the right time. The answer might be, "If I can get you a 10 percent discount, will you put your order in today?" I realize that this is a fairly hard close technique, but if you find yourself being pumped for information, you might throw this in as a last resort. It could be a good method to get your prospect to think about posing other questions with no intention of buying.

This technique works partly because the person who asks the questions is the one who controls the conversation. This is why effective probing is so useful. One reason good probers sell so much on the phone as well as face-to-face is that they control the interview.

On the phone, your interview or probing skills are more important than your approach, presentation, or close. If you can control the conversation by actively listening and asking the right questions in the right way, you will sell.

The prospect's question might be, "When can you deliver it?" Your answer very likely might be, "When do you need it—tomorrow? Yes, I can get it for you tomorrow."

Or he might ask, "Can I get a 10 percent discount?" Your response might be, "If I can get you a 10 percent discount, will you order it today?"

"OK."

"Well, then, I'll give you a 10 percent discount." The added benefit of using closing questions like this is that you're pushing your prospect to commit. He can't say, "Well, I need to run this by my boss for a final decision." If he does, you might say, "I asked you if I could get you a10 percent discount, would you order today? You said yes." The prospect basically has no recourse. He told you he was the decision maker, or at least that he would buy today.

This is an especially good idea for those prospects who call in just to get quotes, like those who call auto-parts stores, hotels, and vacation resorts.

Wouldn't this be an effective technique for hoteliers? Someone might call and say, "How much do you charge for a weekend stay?" The reservation clerk then might say, "When do you want to stay? When do you need the room? You want a 10 percent discount? If I can get you a great discount, are you willing to book it today?"

Think of the business that could be done on the telephone if you avoid being pumped for information and start closing instead. One problem is that clerks fill in the boxes but can't make decisions. As you ask closing questions, the caller will eventually get the decision maker on the phone to talk.

Throughout this section on probing, I've frequently mentioned the high effectiveness of asking the right question at the right time of the right person. I've also discussed effective listening—how you can actually listen people into buying instead of talking them into it.

Probably the best example of this concept of listening people into buying is a story about the late, great sales trainer, Fred Herman. He was the guest on the old *Mike Douglas Show* and was billed as the greatest salesman on earth. Mr. Douglas, feeling very cocky, said to Fred Herman, "Well, you're the greatest. You're the best, right?"

Fred Herman said, "Well, that's what I've been told."

Mike said, "I've decided to set up a little experiment to determine if that's true." He took out a gold inlaid ashtray, and said to Fred, "Sell it to me."

What a question. I can imagine how Fred felt. When I travel around the country speaking, I often chat with fellow travelers. When they find out that I'm a motivational speaker, they say, "Well, motivate me." I feel like laughing in their face and walking off. If they can't motivate themselves, I don't have a prayer. I'm sure this is what Fred Herman felt as Mike Douglas challenged him. What a contrived situation! But what a test of Fred Herman's skill!

Fred looked at the ashtray, picked it up, held it, turned it over, glanced across it, and said to Mike Douglas, "What do you like about this ashtray?"

Mike smiled and said, "Well, it's gold. It's pretty. It's deep. I guess I like that, because I smoke a cigar. The ashes from cigars are fairly thick. I know it could hold a few hours of my smoking. Also, my guests smoke during commercial breaks. I want something I can be proud of to give to them to dump their ashes in."

"How much would you pay for this?"

Mike said, "I don't know, $10, $12." He looked at Fred Herman. Fred looked at Mike and said, "Sold."

Mike laughed and gave him $12.

You see, Fred never presented anything. He asked Mike Douglas what he liked and closed by asking how much he would pay for it. Mike came up with his own benefits, his own price, and bought it.

While you can't let other people tell you how much they want to pay, you certainly can let them tell you what they like best about your product, what the benefits are. This is the whole point behind using the right questions at the right time.

Nine
Reconnecting with Prospects

I recently wrote a column for a popular sales magazine. This column was structured so that I answered questions that were posed to me by emails. I tried to respond to them in as timely a way as possible.

Some of the most interesting questions come from salespeople who have difficulty getting their people to follow up, even those who had responsive and interested prospects on the first call. They often write to me, "I have trouble contacting my prospect. He won't take my phone calls the second time. He cancels my appointments, or when we meet, he lets other people interrupt us and disturb our interview inappropriately." Has this ever happened to you?

The second appointment has a lot to do with what you said in the first appointment. You can cause your prospect to be a lot more committed if you follow a seven-step process. This technique will ensure that the prospect not only sees you a second time but will also put more value in your phone interview and will help him be more receptive to you.

1. After the phone call, make sure you thank your prospect for her time. Let that person know how appreciative you are to let you take his time, as well as how much you appreciate his sharing information with you. Make it sincere. The more candid that prospect is, the more appreciative you should be. Often this technique will cause him to be even more candid. When he's more candid, he may develop greater rapport and trust in you.

2. Arrange for a meeting at the end of the first phone call. Don't let your prospect stall you. Don't let him say, "I'll call you back in a couple of days to arrange a meeting. My secretary is away from her desk right now." Calendar a firm time for follow-up. At least push for a tentative meeting if nothing else. If they insist on calling you and won't book an appointment, you're done.

   Let your prospect know how important another follow-up phone call or a face-to-face appointment is. Inform him that in order for you to do your job and correctly analyze the information you learned, you need to be able to follow up. Say, "Mr. Jones, I'm going to take the information you shared with me and determine whether I may be of help to you." Or "I'm going to have my staff analyze what we've discussed so that I can be prepared for our next talk."

   In other words, let your prospect or client know that you are going through an enormous amount of work to help him solve his problems. Don't ever let him think that you're just going to wing it. The more prepared you make him think you will be for the next meeting, the more apt he is to respect your time at that meeting.

3. Set an appointment to phone him back or see him face-to-face using an alternative-choice close. (I'll say more about the alternative-choice close later.) Say to your prospect, "I'd like to see you Thursday at 3:35 or Friday at 4:45."

   Did you see the *nonround* numbers I used in mentioning the time? There's a special benefit behind this. Never set an appointment on the hour or half hour. If you set an appointment at an odd time like 3:35, it gives your prospect the impression that you're extremely busy. If he thinks you're a busy person, he's less likely to keep you waiting in his office during a face-to-face appointment and more likely to see you. You will give him the impression that you're fitting him into a very busy schedule.

   Do the same thing with callbacks. If upon a first call you decide that you want to do a follow-up call, tell your prospect, "Would it be OK if I called you at 4:45 on Friday?" This gives your prospect the idea that you don't enjoy calling people unless there's a purpose for it; you're much too busy to waste your time and theirs. That's why you're calling at a specific time.

4. Make sure to get an alternate time and phone number from your prospect. Once a prospect cancels or puts off an appointment, it's very difficult to get an appointment back. It's especially difficult to get callback appointments on the phone.

   To avoid this kind of problem, ask your prospect something like, "Just in case we have trouble reaching each other at 4:45 on Friday, can we talk to each other at 4:45 on Monday instead?" Make sure you have an alternate time to reach that person by telephone just in case.

If you have his work phone number, try to get his cell. If you have his cell, then try to get his work phone number. If you're a stockbroker or an insurance agent or a realtor, this is very appropriate and sometimes even necessary. More importantly, it's a way to qualify your prospect's interest.

When I consulted with Prudential Bache Securities, we taught the brokers that if they qualified and probed their prospects, they should ask for a cell number. If that prospect gives his business number, then you ask for his cell. It further commits him and qualifies his interest. It commits him to following up with you.

5. Try to motivate your prospect to be receptive after he receives written information from you. Most of the time, even though the first phone call went well, and you were able to email information out, your prospect may look for a way to disqualify you. He may look for a way to eliminate you instead of looking for a way that you can help him. Try to avoid letting your prospect disqualify you by forewarning him. Get him to agree not to make a decision based only on material that you send to him. It prevents a reflex response.

   Have you heard this from a prospect? "I read your information over, and it just doesn't fit what I do." Avoid this by saying to your prospect before you send the information, "Mr. Jones, you'll see things in the material I send you that you will like a lot and some that you won't even understand, but promise me now that you won't make a decision until I talk to you again at 4:45 on Friday, OK?" This way you can encourage your prospect to keep an open mind. You're avoiding the risk of letting your prospect make a decision based only on what you sent.

When my prospects want to see a video of me speaking, I know that they will see some material that won't fit with their meeting. I can't make a video for every situation. I always say, "This video is only meant to give you an example of my speaking style. I customize every presentation according to the needs of my clients. That is why you will see material in the video that may not fit you, but the client loved it."

Granted, the prospect is going to have some initial judgment about what you send anyway, but if you forewarn him, he's much more apt to at least talk to you and give you objections rather than avoiding your phone calls and face-to-face meetings.

6. Get your prospect's commitment to follow up with you ahead of time. Make sure your sales cycle is full of trial closes. If your prospect doesn't commit to talk to you further, he may not value your time. Say, "Mr. Jones, I'll send you the brochure in an email on my company. In the meantime, I'll analyze the information you gave me. Then I'd like to spend, oh, about fifteen uninterrupted minutes talking about these ideas we've shared when we next meet, OK?"

   You see, you're constantly building up small agreements by saying to your prospects, "I'd like to get information from you." If he agrees to give it, you say, "Thank you for the information. I think I may be able to help you." He may say, "I hope so. I'd like to decrease my premiums and gain more coverage." Every step along the way, he's gaining more benefits. He'll show his enthusiasm by agreeing also.

So even though you're not yet ready to close, you should still trial-close on booking an appointment. It is just one more close among all the little closes you use during the interview process. The close is a process that lasts from the beginning of the approach to making a decision.

7. I saved the best for the last. Do a postclose. Don't worry about overselling. You're actually putting in an insurance policy that will cause your prospect to stay motivated. Let that prospect know your goal is to come up with answers to help her solve problems.

   Remember your prospect's worry list. Your goal is take items off her worry list. When you do, she will buy from you. Before you get off the telephone, give her a final reason why she should talk to you further on a face-to-face appointment or to keep her telephone appointment with you.

   Do a postclose. Say, "Mr. Jones, when I see you next week, I know that you'll see how this investment will give 10 to 15 percent capital appreciation next year. After we meet next week, Mr. Jones, you'll be very excited about the amount of money this will save you."

   Here you're using a technique to encourage your prospect. Give him confidence that you are going to give him a key benefit that he will be interested in. Because of this, your prospect will very likely want to see you again.

   Always keep in mind that your prospect is much more interested in himself than in you or your product. If you tell her what he'll get by talking to you a second time, he's much more apt to keep a second appointment.

Other information that you need to uncover during the probing process are the various steps of the decision process. Among every decision a prospect makes are a series of steps that she uses to determine whether she will buy. Sometimes it's complex and entails a number of different decision strategies. At other times, it's just a simplistic yes or no. From start to finish, from an introductory phone call to delivery of the product, you must learn exactly what has to happen to help your prospect decide whether or not she wants to buy your product.

Learning Your Prospect's Decision Strategy

If you would like to learn your prospect's decision strategy, ask this question: "Mr. Prospect, I'm going to email you some information as you requested, but out of curiosity, what will happen after that?"

He may say, "I'll get together with my assistant, and we'll decide if your cloud system is appropriate for our needs." Or he may say, "I'll take it to my executive board and see if they would like to authorize an expenditure of this type."

Another step you might ask about is the length of time. "Mr. Prospect, after you have decided to move on this, how long will it take? After you get the information, what will happen then? After you talk to your assistant, what will happen then?" If you get specific enough with the prospect, he is bound to be specific with you. He will undoubtedly respect your wishes and tell you what he wants you to know.

Recently a meeting planner used some of my techniques to sell her services to Lincoln National in the Midwest. She asked for her prospect's decision steps. She said to him on the phone, "What's the first step in deciding whether to use me as a meeting planner for your company's next convention?"

The prospect said, "Number one, we have to determine where the convention is going to be."

"What next?"

"We have to figure out the theme for the convention."

"What next then?"

"The time slots for all the speakers, the hotel, date; finally get the president to OK it."

In just a few short minutes, she was able to find most of the pieces of information she needed to determine what he was going to go through in using her as a meeting planner. This is very important, since many meetings cost in excess of $400,000 to put on, even for small conferences. Meeting planners often take 15–25 percent of the meeting cost, possibly netting her an enormous amount of money. So she really needed to use her head and ask the right questions.

Ten

Key Words and Phrases

Have you ever noticed a prospect using words that you don't usually use in your own vocabulary? Have you heard certain jargon terms or usage that may even seem unique? These usages are called *key words.*

When you ask questions about whether a prospect is a candidate for your service, you will hear them use certain words that possess a vast amount of meaning to them. These key words give you information about how your prospect thinks. If you want to generate rapport, you must learn your their jargon and key words.

If you were to talk to me on the phone, I would use my own key words and phrases. These words reflect the meaning of a lot of what I say. Since I played professional tennis, I tend to use tennis-based terms in normal conversation. For example, I say things like, "I was able to ace that group." This means it was practically a perfect speech. If everybody enjoyed it, I might say, "The speech was a winner." This means I really got to them. They respected and enjoyed what I had to say. Another of my key words is to say, "I double-faulted." This means I made a critical error and lost the business.

If you use those key words in selling to me, I'll be all over you like a cheap suit, because those words and phrases convey meaning in my own vocabulary. In selling your products, don't make your prospect learn your words. Instead, learn their words. They will buy from you much more quickly. Using your prospect's own key words is like talking their language. It gains you more trust and rapport.

You've heard that a picture is worth 1000 words. Well, your prospect's key words and phrases are worth 2000 pictures. Your prospect will let you know when they are using key words also. They'll pause directly before they say it as well as afterward. I once worked with a company executive who kept describing his corporate bureaucracy as a "puzzle palace." Every time I talked about confusion in management, I'd say, "Those people are probably in a puzzle palace." He always knew what I meant.

In the financial-services industry, when you want to get across the point that something will be a benefit, you might say, "It will generate return."

In the 1980s, George Shultz, Ronald Reagan's secretary of state, also used key words. He would say things like, "Gorbachev and I had substantive talks." If you could have found out what "substantive talks" meant and used it when you sold George Shultz, he may have bought a few missiles from you.

Sometimes key words are not that obvious. Sometimes they're much subtler. For my audio program "Sales Magic: How to Double Production," I did an in-depth study on new research on how people think.

Your prospects and clients are broken up into three basic modes: those who see, those who hear, and those who feel. The individuals who see use sight-based visual words, like *see*, *clear*, *picture*, *perspec-*

tive, and *view*. People who hear use words like *sound*, *tone*, *hear*, *key*, *reverberate*, and others that reflect sound. People who feel use words like *feel*, *impression*, *rub*, *grab*, and *touch base*.

Visuals say things like, "Yes, I *see* what you mean." "Let me give you my *perspective*." "Here's my *view*." "It's *clear* to me so far."

Sound-based people use sentences like, "How does this *sound* to you?" "Does that *ring a bell*?" "Can you *key into* what I'm talking about?" "Do you *hear* what I'm saying?" My mother used to say, "Kerry, don't take that *tone* with me, young man."

Feeling-based people might say, "Let me give you my *impression*. Here's how I *feel* about it? How does it *rub* you? Let's *touch base* next week."

If you can gain access to frequently used words such as these, you'll also gain access to your prospect's mind. One technique you might use is to match their key words. With a visual you might say, "Does this look good to you?" With sound people you might say, "How does this sound to you?" With feeling people, you might use words such as, "How do you feel about this?"

A partner with an accounting company, Deloitte Consulting, received a call from a credit-union executive. Because of tax-law changes, the executive wanted the Deloitte rep, Larry, to speak at a conference. He wanted to screen Larry on the phone by asking questions about how he would handle himself at the conference if he were to speak.

Larry wanted the gig. Speaking at a conference like that would mean an enormous source of future clients for him. The executive said, "I'd like to know your *view* on how you would handle this. I'd like to get your *perspective* on what you would show the audience. Can you let me *see* a little bit of what your lecture would *look like*?"

Larry realized on the spot that this person was a visual. He then said, "I'd like to send you my handouts for attendees. Blue handouts with gray borders, how does that look to you?"

The prospect said, "Wonderful."

"To give you a better perspective on my PowerPoint slides, I'll send you these slides in an email so we can look at them right now if you want."

The prospect said, "It looks good to me."

Larry accessed that individual's sight-based mind by using visual words when he communicated. Larry picked up business by using key words. If you use this concept in the right way with the right person, you also will pick up business that you wouldn't normally get.

Eleven

The Presentation

So far you've learned how to approach your prospect or client and get through the secretarial screen to the decision maker. You have also learned how to use a script to become more articulate and prepared on the telephone. You've additionally learned how to probe to find out your prospect and client's needs.

In this chapter, we'll not only cover how to present your product or service ideas, but more importantly, how to present those ideas in the way your prospect wants to buy. This section on presenting is probably the one that's talked about the most by sales trainers coast to coast.

The difference is that on the phone you have to be able to present your ideas more concisely and succinctly, using each word to grab your prospect. Unlike a face-to-face interview, you can't talk indirectly about benefits, hoping your prospect will suddenly buy them. In a face-to-face interview, you can use a shotgun approach. This is much more difficult on the telephone, where you have to rifle-shot the product benefit in exactly the way your prospect wants to perceive it. If you do this, you will make a sale.

The first rule of presenting on the telephone is not just explaining your ideas but selling them. Most salespeople from coast to coast explain and try to educate. They typically answer questions and explain the technical makeup of the product. This will help your prospects find out a lot more about your product than they previously knew, but won't put any dollars in your pocket.

I have a friend who sold annuities—an insurance product. We had her over for Christmas Day at a family reunion recently. She enjoyed talking to prospects but felt uncomfortable pushing them. I helped her realize that she wasn't really pushing her prospects as much as helping them reach a decision. I explained something all sharp phone salespeople understand: if you only educate your prospects, they will buy from somebody else, but if you present the product in terms of what the prospect needs and wants, they will see it as a benefit and buy.

Often during the probing stage, your prospects will share their needs and desires. They'll tell you their wants and will often let you know whether they can benefit from your product. All you have to do then is simply match their needs to your product's benefits. But few salespeople understand that if they present more benefits than the prospect wants to hear, the prospect may lose interest. The salesperson may blow himself right out of the sale. This happens all too frequently. Salespeople often feel they have to explain the product or service to the point that the prospect becomes bored or even disinterested.

It's a little like the young boy who went to his father one day and said, "Dad, where did I come from?" The father, realizing this was "the time," explained about procreation for a solid two hours. The father then said to the boy, "Do you understand all this?" The boy said, "Yes, Dad, I do, but Jimmy came from Detroit, and I just want to know where I came from."

You may be explaining a whole lot more than your prospect wants to hear. There's a popular saying in the professional speaking business: the only way a speaker can say less is to speak longer.

If you get one thing from this chapter on presenting on the phone, it should be to present those product benefits that answer your prospect's needs. Avoid the temptation to tell your prospect everything. Keep your mouth shut.

Once I consulted with a financial planner. During an interview, my client asked his client what he most wanted to gain from investments. The client said, "I want growth and cash flow." The financial planner then presented a few limited partnerships. He discussed growth and cash flow, but also mutual funds, annuities, stocks, and bonds. He presented basically three times as much as the prospect was interested in. You could see confusion and frustration on the prospect's face. Although the prospect was polite and didn't try to interrupt the planner, that sale was lost within the first ten minutes.

Here's a key idea for you. The better job you do on the telephone in matching your product benefits to the information you received during the probing stage, the fewer objections you will receive when you try to close. This means a lot, because it states that the better you listen during the probing or fact-finding stage, the more committed your prospect will be to buying your product.

Think for a moment. What are the features of a mechanical pencil? It has an eraser on the end. It has lead that sticks out of the tip without the need to be sharpened. It is also durable and lasts a lot longer than a regular pencil. But there's a big difference between the features I just named and the benefits.

The *features* of a mechanical pencil are the characteristics that make it salable. The *benefits* of the pencil are how those features help the prospect.

The benefits of an eraser on a mechanical pencil are that it allows me to quickly and easily get rid of mistakes without leaving a trace. The benefit of a clicker is to advance the lead smoothly without sharpening. Another benefit of the mechanical pencil is durability: I won't have to go and buy a new pencil very often. The pencil fits nicely into my hand. It's not as thin as most pencils, thereby enabling me to write for longer periods of time without fatigue.

Effectively presenting product benefits is more important on the telephone than it is face-to-face, because you have less time to probe and present. It's critical to focus on listening. The more benefits you can match to your prospect's needs, the quicker you'll be able to sell.

There are two kinds of benefits: primary and secondary. A primary benefit is totally dependent on your prospect's needs. It's your prospect's most important need, such as the ability to advance the lead, or an eraser that lasts for a long time. You can only learn what the primary benefit is by asking the prospects what their most important needs are.

A secondary benefit is also important, but it is lower down on the priority ladder—for example, the width of a mechanical pencil. It feels good in my hand, but it's not as important as the clicker, which advances the lead. The color of the mechanical pencil could be secondary. It's important for aesthetic reasons, but could take second place to a primary benefit, such as that of an eraser. Again, it is impossible to know a product benefit until you first find out what the prospect wants. Which features are beneficial?

Have you ever seen the commercial on television selling Hanes underwear? Have you seen inspector number 12? She's a woman in her late fifties, and her sole job is to inspect men's briefs. Her line is, "It doesn't say *Hanes* until *I* say it says *Hanes*." The same is true of a product benefit. It doesn't say *benefit* until your prospect *says* it says benefit.

I was recently called by a woman selling conference-call discount services. She didn't ask any questions at all during the conversation, but her approach was good, so I listened for three or four minutes. She told me about her Webex type of service. It was with a nationwide company, and she explained that the discount would be between 10 and 30 percent below Webex. She also said I could use an 800 number to access the call line and then dial in my unique code. I would also have individualized statements depending on the code number used.

After she was done, I said, "Thank you very much. I'm not interested." I was interested in a discount bridge-line service, but I was not interested in her product features. I'd been using join.me for a few years. I was not especially loyal but was looking for a better deal. I was interested in making a change, but I did not need her product features. I did need her to listen to my needs and to match how her features with them, explaining what could have been beneficial to me. If she had taken some time to probe, she would have known what features to present and then translated those into benefits. If she knew what you know now about features and benefits, she would have said, "Do you travel a lot?"

Of course I'd say, "Yes, I do."

Then she would have said, "Do you ever travel to more rural areas or just to major cities?"

"Both."

"It might be beneficial to you to use our toll-free access code. Whether you're in Podunk, Iowa, or Chicago, Illinois, or even abroad, your clients can call in toll-free. Will that work?" That would have been very beneficial.

She could have said, "Would you like to know just how much it's costing you right now to use your current vendor versus us?" I would have said yes to that.

She then could have explained to me that I could get an itemized statement depending on the access code used. She would have discovered that the international toll-free number was more important to me than the itemized statements. This primary benefit probably would have sold me on its own, without her presenting the secondary, itemized-statement benefit.

I live and work in Portugal one month per quarter. I have to dial in two sets of Skype numbers followed by two sets of conference-call numbers. Dialing fewer numbers is really important to me. But she never asked.

Make sure that when you do present your product benefits, you support your statements. Prove what you say. Make supporting statements that your prospect can understand. If you sell mutual funds, make sure you cite independent reports from *Financial Service Times* magazine or *Research* magazine. Show that your fund is number one in the country. Pull out a copy of *Money* magazine, which rated your fund as number one last year, with an average growth rate of a net asset value of 8 percent.

There are three things to do after you present product benefits. Number one is to prove it. Number two is to prove it. Guess what number three is—prove it. If you can prove benefits exactly when your prospect wants to hear about them, you will keep your prospect in agreement most of the time. If you can keep your prospect in agreement with you most or all of the time, you'll save a lot of time and cut down the sales cycle.

I had a phone conversation with the regional director for a very large financial-products firm that sold products through stockbrokers. They were evaluating whether to use me to help their brokers increase their closing ratios. At one point, I told him on the telephone that if his firm sponsored me to speak at this company's regional conferences, he would generate more loyalty as the brokers increased sales.

I mentioned the feature that using me would increase sales. But he said a few minutes earlier that throwing cocktail parties and sponsoring golf tournaments did nothing for increasing business. When I mentioned loyalty as a product benefit, he became skeptical. (You really can determine a lot by silence during a phone conversation.)

I immediately made a supporting statement. I read two lines from a letter from a company president who also used me for conferences. I had given a speech in Tahiti sponsored by another company. The president of this firm specifically mentioned in his letter that his salespeople increased the company's sales and had paid for my appearance.

This grabbed my prospect's attention. He became much more excited about using me, thinking he could get the same benefit. In other words, I incorporated supporting proof when talking about the benefit he would receive from using my services.

There are three things your prospect thinks about when you present solutions and benefits. They will either help make or break a phone sale. Number one is need, number two is money, and number three is urgency. Nearly all your prospect's objections are based on these three issues. whether they voice them or not. That is, "I have no need, I have no money, and I'm in no hurry."

When there is no need, it's tough to sell anything. The objective is to convince your prospect they actually need or, better yet, want your product. How do you this? It's very simple. Madison Avenue has spent enormous amounts of money trying to convince us that we need to put a filmy substance underneath our arms to keep from smelling bad. But if you're clean and take a bath every day, chances are others won't be able to smell you.

A few years ago, an ad campaign ran trying to let people know that they actually had bad breath. Employees of companies would try to figure out how they could tell the boss his breath was unbearable. The ad even went so far as to let consumers know that if they told the offending boss he had breath, they'd get fired.

In one commercial, two furniture movers walking up a staircase with a piano displayed this concern. One worker on the lower side of the piano told his friend he had bad breath. His friend let the piano fall, rolling over the other worker as it slid down the staircase. This was Madison Avenue's attempt to say if you tell someone they have bad breath, they may feel insulted. You just have to know when your breath is bad, because no one else will tell you. In this way, you can create a perceived need. If you can convince your prospect in order to help them achieve their goals, they need your product (in this case mouthwash), they will buy.

In a similar example, a discount cloud-storage salesperson tried to convince me that if my goal was to save money on data storage, I needed to have his system to accomplish my objectives. This often works fairly well. Again, in order to find out whether your prospect needs your service, you must first find out their goals and objectives. Then you can provide a solution.

The second roadblock your prospect will create is, "I don't have any money." Your prospect is constantly trying to convince himself that your product is too expensive. Every prospect thinks the same thing. They spent too much money already and don't want to spend any more.

Recently I did a screening-first appointment with coaching prospect. Within the first five minutes, he said he couldn't afford my fees. I asked what he thought my coaching fees were. He said, "Too much." Without establishing value, everything is too expensive.

Again Madison Avenue has eased the impact of the money problem. They say, "You can pay over the next 30 years. You won't have to pay until February." An easier ploy is to convince your prospect that they have money for things that are important. (Sure, you can offer credit terms, but today it may not make that much of a difference.) As I mentioned earlier, it's very likely your prospect has more money than time. In other words, making your product easy to use and get may mean more than making it cheaper.

The third roadblock to your presentation success is your prospect's attitude of "I'm not in hurry." Have you heard this before? "I don't have to make a decision right now. Let me go think about it."

This is probably the worst objection, because it's such a reflex response: it is said automatically without much thought. For example, you might visit a clothing store. The salesperson says, "Can I help you?" Your automatic reflex response is, "No thanks, I am just looking."

A reflex response is when your prospect tries to put off any and all purchases until he can't live without it, or until it is laid in his lap with no effort and little charge.

I once consulted with a banking firm in California. One of the officers told me there are three variables one tries to attain during a business transaction—price, timing, and quality. Unfortunately, you can never have all three. At best you will get two. If you want a great price, you have to relinquish getting it now and getting the best service available. Or you can pay now and get it later, with a lower price and great quality.

Have you ever thought about what you're really getting when you buy a $800 color TV? If you want your product today, it's more difficult to get an 89 percent discount with top quality. On the other hand, if you want the best quality available, you'll pay more for it as well as possibly taking longer to get it.

Many advertisers these days are saying, "Our product cost a few dollars more, but the quality is worth it." Chevy Volt advertises that high-quality theme: you pay a few more dollars now, but you'll get better quality when you buy our product. They suggest the price is mitigated by the quality and long-term savings. The fuel savings with this electric car will make up for the higher cost.

Let your prospect know that you want to give him price, quality, and timing, but he must work with you to get the two of the three he wants most. If he wants it now, make him understand that you will try to accommodate him, but the price will go up unless he buys right away. Scarcity sets in. In other words, whether it's true or not that the price will increase, prevent your prospect from procrastinating by giving him the illusion that you will not be able to hold the price where it is.

In my business, my speaking fee will increase whenever I think the demand for my service gets too high, or I am limited in how many times a month I want to speak. I will often decrease or negotiate my speaking fee when I have too little business. A great way of controlling the number of speeches I give around the country is controlling the price.

Often large corporations can't do this because their overhead is too high. One technique that I frequently use in with seminar program chairs is to use time limits. For example, they may possibly feel that my speaking fee of $10,000 is too high for them. They would like me to decrease my price to $7500 for the presentation.

I'm often inclined to say yes, but I'll also add, "I'll hold that price for you, but only for one day. Can you make a decision that fast?" I will never guarantee a price for more than a twenty-four-hour period of time. In other words, I'm giving that person one of the two—price or time.

If you're selling paper clips, you could tell the prospect that if he buys right now, you'll pay the shipping. If you're trying to book an appointment to review an insurance policy, you can build in value by saying, "If we can meet within the next week, I'll analyze your policy free of charge. If we wait past next week, I may not have enough time. My staff will have the time to it now. Past that, it will be harder to get to it."

You can even negotiate little things in your product or service to overcome the no-need, no-money, no-urgency problems. If you understand these three roadblocks and work ways to overcome them into your closing presentation, you'll be able to sell by gently pushing your prospect during this stage.

Try to negotiate with your prospects. Get them to buy now for goals they want to achieve. But remember, price is not the only objective.

Rephrasing and Reconfirming

Do you usually do a good job of probing your prospect's needs and wants? If you do, it's very important to reconfirm those needs before you start presenting your product. Not only will it help you keep your presentation focused on their needs, but it will remind them of what you heard them say and the most important aspects of what they told you. If you don't, you may simply generate instant objections or oversell when they hear you present benefits they don't want.

Let me give you an example. A regional director of a very large company called me to ask whether I would be available to speak to his managers. I asked what he thought would be best to include in my presentation. He mentioned that he wanted a speaker who would help his managers get inside the heads of their salespeople to help produce more.

I listened to the manager talk for about seven or eight minutes. Then I rephrased some of the things I heard him say. "Ed, you mentioned you wanted a speaker who could help your managers get inside the heads of their salespeople, right? You also want the speaker to help the managers develop their salespeople so they could increase production." To my incredible surprise, he said, "No, that's not what I meant." He gave me another seven or eight minutes on what he thought he meant to say rather than what I had heard. If I had simply starting presenting the benefits of using me as a speaker after listening to what he said initially, I would have lost that business. It would have been as bad as not listening to him at all.

When reconfirming your prospect's needs, the rule of thumb is to realize it's not the prospect's responsibility to get you to understand their needs. It's up to you to understand what their needs are by getting inside their head. This means that two people can attach totally different meanings to the same words. It also means that your prospect may understand something completely different from the same words that you do.

Here are some steps to help you reconfirm your prospect's needs before you start the presentation cycle. First, rephrase what was said in your own words directly after your prospect says them. This should be done every seven to ten minutes. If you wait too long, you may forget too much of what he said or incorrectly write down what you heard.

Second, remember to write down your prospect's key words and phrases. It's very important to know that when your prospect says, "I want to give you *my* business," it's very different from saying, "I want to give you *the* business." *The* business could mean problems, hassles, and grief. *My* business could mean fees for doing work with my company.

After you're done rephrasing what your prospect said in your own words, ask, "Mr. Jones, is this what you meant to say?" He will in turn quickly tell you the real meaning behind his words. One problem is that not only are salespeople poor listeners, but they also present solutions to needs they never understood; they only hear the words that come out of the prospect's mouth. They attach their own meaning to what the prospect said rather than trying to understand what the prospect meant.

Use these three techniques to rephrase:

1. Remember key words and ask about meaning before you start any presentation cycle. For example, say, "I heard you say that you want to increase your income. What do you mean by that?"
2. Start every conversation by reminding your prospect of what they said and what you thought they meant. Act as if your prospect on the telephone is the most unique prospect or client you've ever had. Let him know that you're prepared to provide solutions to their needs. This is especially important if you're sending out follow-up letters and email.
3. Make sure that when you reconfirm a telephone conversation, rephrase what your prospect said about their needs before you try to recommend or present your product or service. This will give your prospect the reason behind your recommendations. It will give them a framework for attaching more benefits to your presentation.

In my office, we have a rule: we always reconfirm past conversations at the start of the second telephone call. This is especially effective if we have not talked to prospects in a couple of weeks or months. It reminds them of what they said initially; more importantly, it lets them know what we understood from the last conversation. Sometimes we're wrong about the prospect's needs. More often, we're correct. We take great pains in reconfirming past conversations, or even what was said, in an effort to avoid miscommunication and losing a sale. This is probably the single most important thing we do in making follow-up phone calls.

We try to avoid making a cold call to a prospect we've already spoken to. A prospect is very apt to forget about past calls unless he is reminded of the initial conversation.

During the probing section, you heard how to find out your prospect's decision strategy or how he will decide to buy. The question to discover this was, "How did you decide to buy last time?" The prospect is likely to say, "Oh, he gave me a great price. It also had very good durability. I like the reputation from the supplier."

In this case, when you present the product benefits, it's OK to cover the various aspects of service: quality, reputation, the length of time the company has been in existence, the number of salespeople, the service contract. But make sure you focus on the price, the durability of the product, and the reputation of the company. Your prospect may pay attention other things you say, but approximately 80 percent of the reason they'll buy will have to do with those three needs. Your presentation should be focused almost completely on what you heard during the probing phase. Center primarily on their buying strategy.

Remember when we discussed your prospects' various thought patterns? Do you recall that we called some of your prospects sight-based people? They use words like, "I *see* what you're talking about. It's *clear.* I can *picture* that. Here's my *perspective.*" Hearing-based prospects use words like, "*Sounds* good. It *rings a bell.* I like that *tone.* I like what I'm *hearing* so far." Feeling-based prospects use words like, "Let's *touch base* next week. I *feel* that I understand it. It *grabs* me. Here's my *impression.*"

Most sophisticated phone salespeople are able to reach out and rifle-shot their product's benefits into their prospects' minds by using key words. If your prospect is primarily a sight-based buyer, you might say, "If you consider buying a dozen of these parts, Mr. Jones, I think you'll *see* a big discount. How does that *look* to you so far?"

If your phone prospect is hearing-based, you might say, "I might be able to lower your premiums if we can *talk* next week. How does Thursday at 4:45 or Friday at 5:15 *sound* to you, Mr. Prospect? I'm sure you *hear* promises from other salespeople, but I have an idea that I know will want to *hear.*"

For feeling-based prospects, you might say, "I want you to *feel* good about our company. You'll *feel* comfortable with our service. I hope your *impression* of us after you've used our product for a while will be one of comfort, Mr. Prospect."

Can you see how these modes of sight, hearing, and feeling can be used to present your service? If you work at presenting your product or service in the mode your prospect wants, you'll be way ahead of the game.

Don't assume all your prospects are picture people. Approximately 35 percent of your prospects are sight-based, 25 percent are hearing-based, and 40 percent are feeling-based. While you can see, hear, and feel at any time you want, there is one mode through which you are likely to buy. It's like being right-handed. If your prospect is right-handed, she's perfectly able to use her left hand whenever she wants, but she is much more likely to use her right hand than the left. She's more comfortable with her right hand than with the left. The same thing is true of your prospect's mental thought patterns. If you're aware of these, you'll cause your prospect to be much more comfortable on the phone and help her buy more quickly.

The Reference Sell

Would you like to know the strongest technique you can use in presenting your product on the telephone? This has to be the best way of proving that your benefits are truly the ones that will help your prospect accomplish their goals. It's called the *reference sell*. It's truly the strongest way of selling your benefits.

If you talk about the companies or people who are using your service and how they're using it, you will be more persuasive because of the reference and endorsement. When using a reference sell, make sure the people or companies you talk about are ones your prospect recognizes or should recognize. They could be in the same business or industry. You can make it more powerful by mentioning the name of the person in the company. Also, be as specific as possible about how they applied it. Don't just talk about a client who bought your service. Instead talk about how they used it. Mention their names and what they looked like. The best producers will even tell a story.

I recently spoke to a large insurance company, US Life. Bill, the VP of sales, wanted to use me for a conference in Las Vegas. I listened to Bill and probed for his needs during lunch.

Directly after, I decided to do a reference sell. I pulled out a recommendation letter from Jim Pack, president of Provident Life. Both of these companies were alike in how they sold.

When I mentioned Provident, Bill perked up. He asked me questions about what I did for Provident. By using this reference sell, I generated much more interest than I could have from fifteen minutes of talking. I became much more credible and believable: one of his competitors was already using me successfully to achieve their goals.

Joy on my staff often used a reference sell. When she first started, I spent almost two solid weeks helping her memorize the various companies I had done business with as well as the magazines I wrote for. When she called a prospect on the phone who had not heard of me, she mentioned those companies by saying, "Dr. Johnson writes monthly for *Broker World* and *Financial Service Times*, as well as *Business to Business* on topics like 'How to Read Your Client's Mind' and 'Sales Magic.'" When they heard the magazines, they felt as if they should know me. Joy was able to gain more rapport and credibility on the phone.

In the following example, try to guess what mode the prospect is using, and listen for the reference sell.

KERRY: Jan, I'd like to be considered as a speaker at your April conference.

JAN: Well, we usually use technical speakers only. Our people tell us they only listen to speakers who will broaden their product-information base.

KERRY: I understand you use only technical speakers. Will James with Integrated Resources said the same thing to me. He also said his attendees thought my presentation helped them increase their sales by using more effective people skills. Does that sound like an idea that might work for your group?

JAN: Yes, let's talk more about that.

Story Selling

Would you like to find a way to get your prospect or client to more quickly understand your benefits and remember them longer? In doing our two-year study with some of the most successful phone salespeople, we noticed some striking similarities. The most effective of these producers have an uncanny way of getting their prospects to understand the products very quickly by using stories and metaphors. They can get the prospect to fantasize about potential benefits. They get their prospects to identify with using the products to solve problems and implement solutions. They give them a real person to identify with who had this problem or used this product.

Let me give you an example. My financial advisor back in the 1980s was Dennis Renter from Newport Beach, California. Dennis was in the midst of discussing a real-estate limited partnership. In those days, I had a life's ambition to sail around the world on a yacht.

I told Dennis I was unsure about the partnership. Dennis did know that I wanted something with a very high return but that was not speculative. He suggested a mutual fund with a timing service. The way stock-market timing worked was to put money in the fund when it goes up and take money out and into a more stable money-market account when the fund's assets went down. This going in and out of the fund without incurring sales charges is the essence of timing. The theory was to double the annual returns of a normal mutual fund.

I was only slightly interested in this idea. Then Dennis told me about a current client who had a forty-foot sailboat. That got me really interested. He described the boat, and I immediately realized it was a ketch made by a company I recognized. Dennis told me that his two older teenagers and his wife were sailing around the islands of Tahiti. He said they had been gone for about eighteen months and planned on staying for at least three more years on their trip. He talked about the postcards and letters he received from the client and how much he appreciated Dennis taking over their financial-investing responsibilities. The client also bragged about the great return Dennis was generating. The gain of approximately 12 to 15 percent on all their investments enabled the family to continue sailing around the world.

Dennis couldn't have been any more persuasive. He got me salivating about that mutual fund and its timing service. That was exactly the kind of life I wanted to lead. As Dennis told me that story, my interest skyrocketed.

You can use storytelling most effectively to explain product benefits. It's also a way of pushing your prospect to act more quickly.

Another incredibly good technique is to use metaphors. Top pros making more than $1 million a year are incredibly good at using the prospect's own words to sell their services and products.

For example, I'm often asked as I speak around the country if I dislike traveling. If I'm speaking to a sales group, I often say, "Well, of course, I don't like traveling, but you probably don't like cold-calling either." In that way, I directly associate what it's like to travel a lot to something salespeople don't like to do, but sometimes must. It's a necessary evil. The person who asked me the question got a very quick idea of what it was like and immediately understood what I meant. This immediate understanding and comprehension makes metaphors so incredibly effective.

Burt Meisel, an insurance sales pro in Detroit, was phenomenal at this. Whether he was selling an insurance policy over the phone or just trying to book an appointment, he always tried to work metaphors into the conversation. If Burt was talking to a carpeting retailer, he might say, "Mr. Jones, the difference between whole-life and term is like the difference between indoor and outdoor carpeting. One lasts a whole lot longer and is much more plush." That business owner knows immediately what the difference is. Burt knew right away which product was right for the prospect and how to communicate it. He also attached immediate benefits.

Thirty years ago, a discount telephone-service salesperson called and asked if I had an autodialer on my telephone. I said yes. She said, "Our service is easy to use." She then pushed one button on her autodialer. From my experience with my own automatic dialer, I immediately knew how quickly and easily I would be able to dial a special-access code to use her service.

The only way to use metaphors, stories, and analogies is to first learn about your prospect's business and personal life. When you learn something about them, you can tailor these advanced techniques to them. But if you just give a canned presentation, you'll be doomed to rejection with a low closing ratio.

Tie-Downs

Would you like to learn a technique that will keep your prospect in agreement as you present ideas? That technique is called *tie-downs*. It is a psychological method by which you try to get your prospect to agree during every statement you make. You are throwing in affirmative questions at the end of each statement to grab your prospect's interest.

This technique is even more important on the phone than it is face-to-face. In person, you might say, "This will help you, won't it?"

Your prospect may suddenly nod their head up and down and smile. But on the phone, you may not know whether the head nods up and down or not. That's why it's important to get a response to your telephone questions with a tie-down.

One big benefit of tie-downs is that they keep your prospect participating during the presentation cycle. If you talk *at* your prospect, you won't know whether they are with you, against you, in agreement, or negative. They may be waiting for you to stop talking before they hang up.

Here's how tie-downs work: give a feature, translate it into a benefit, and ask a rhetorical question. Tie-downs demand a quick response. For example, "I bet that a quick delivery will help you meet your deadline, won't it? "This discount for ordering in the next twenty-four hours will help you stay on budget, do you agree?" "Shorter delivery time will get this in your staff's hands faster, won't it?" "Because our master-charge imprinter is small, it'll be lighter in your bag, correct?" You should be able to use tie-downs like these to keep your prospect interacting and participating during the presentation.

Say It/Ask It

One way of presenting your product benefits without manipulation is called the *say it/ask it* technique. I personally like this better than the tie-down because it enables you to interact sincerely and authentically with the prospect about the ideas you present. It allows the prospect to let you know whether a feature is really a benefit or not. It enables him to tell you on the spot whether he thinks that feature is important and how he can use it. It puts the prospect in the control seat, letting you know what he likes and dislikes.

Again, it's important to keep the prospect participating. The rule in selling on the phone is never to allow yourself to speak more than fifteen seconds at a time without getting that prospect's reaction, comments, feedback, and response. This will stop you from talking too long. It will also help you decrease objections. The worst objections will come when your prospect isn't able to participate. This rule will also help you tailor your benefits directly to what your prospect wants in the first place. More importantly, it will help your prospect buy more quickly.

Here's an example of the say it/ask it technique: "We offer twenty-four-hour delivery, Mr. Jones. Is prompt delivery important to you? I'm willing to give you a 10 percent discount, Mr. Jones. Is saving money important to you right now? We provide a one-year, no-question warranty on this. You mentioned that a solid warranty is important. Is that still right?"

This last example is probably the best use of the say it/ask it technique. You're confirming what the prospect said he wanted in the first place by saying, "We provide a one-year, no-question warranty on this." Then you reconfirmed that the warranty is important to him by saying, "You mentioned that a solid warranty is important to you, right?" This prevents a bad objection from popping up. The prospect will tell you on the spot what he likes and doesn't.

Whatever service you sell, make sure you use the say it/ask it technique. You will solve lots of problems and decrease objections by using this very valuable concept. Here's an example of how the say it/ask it technique might work for you.

KERRY: Our real-estate company is doing free home analysis this month for any homeowner who is interested in learning the value of their property. Would you like to know how much your house is worth right now?

KEVIN: How long will it take?

KERRY: Oh, between fifteen and thirty minutes. Is that quick enough for you?

KEVIN: Yes, I guess so.

KERRY: I'll be by on Tuesday at 4:10. Is that a good time for you?

KEVIN: Make it 4:30. I'll be back from an appointment then.

KERRY: OK. I'll also bring you information on what other houses have sold for in your neighborhood. Would you be interested in the comps from your neighborhood?

KEVIN: Yes, bring those also.

Trial Closing

We haven't reached the section on how to close yet, but I'd like to ask you a question: when is the best time to close? It's not at the end, nor is it at the beginning, although both those answers are absolutely correct.

The best time to close is early, late, and as often in between as possible. Closing, in my opinion, should be made part of the presentation. Why not close when your prospect wants to buy rather than when you want to sell? Let your prospect say yes. You will be very surprised at how quickly they will buy. Why wait until you want to sell?

One element of effective closing is called *trial closing*. This will help your prospect make a conclusive commitment even before he has actually decided to sign the contract. The best time to trial-close is during your presentation.

I've already mentioned that I'm often solicited by my college alumni association. Once in a while, the telemarketer does a fantastic job. Other times, they're awful.

Recently, an alumni-association member approached, bridged to qualify, and then probed. She said, "Dr. Johnson, the money that you send in will be used for research, housing, maintenance materials, and new construction. At the $1,000 level, you have the choice between focusing your donation for research or new construction. Where would you like your money to go?" Another time she said, "Did you think your college experience was a useful one that would benefit another student?"

In both cases, she was trial-closing. She was trying to get me to make small commitments during the presentation in an effort to make the bigger close at the end easier. Since I'd been agreeing with her continuously, I couldn't help but say yes to her at the end.

A technique I frequently use to trial-close is to get a tentative date for a speaking engagement. The program chair or meeting planner will often say, "Kerry, why don't you just send me written information?"

In my business, sending a demo video is probably a good idea, since meeting planners don't often book speakers they haven't seen or heard before. I usually trial-close by saying, "I'd be glad to send that. By the way, when is your next conference?" They'll often give me a date, say April 18. I then say, "I'm going to pencil this date into my calendar so that we both have a target to shoot for. Is that OK?"

In this way, I'm actually trial-closing the prospect. If they say, "It's too early to do that," I have to go back to probing to find out what they really wanted. On the other hand, if they say, "Sure that's fine," they are in effect saying, "I have tentatively decided to use you. It's not firm yet. But so far everything seems pretty good. I'm interested, and the commitment may be there later."

One member of my staff, Jamie, trial-closed Joy in our office when she first interviewed for the job. I was very impressed, since Jamie has apparently no sales experience except as a retail clerk in a clothing store. But after the interview Jamie said, "What do you think about me? Do you think I might be a contribution to the business?"

This may seem very simplistic, but for someone with no previous sales experience compared to the other people that we interviewed, we all thought that it refreshing that Jamie tried to receive a preliminary decision. Joy said she smiled and said, "I think you'll do just fine." Jamie ended up getting the job and being a super receptionist. One of the best ways to trial-close is simply to ask your prospect's opinion.

Remember, if you do a presentation and don't get constant feedback, your closing ratio will never be high. I recently sat in on an advertising agency's presentation to one of my major clients. They listened and probed fairly well before they presented. They had a flip chart as well as a slide presentation, complete with drawings illustrating the TV ad concepts.

The presentation went on for almost an hour when the client was asked what they thought. The client hemmed and hawed and soon said no. Your prospect or client should never reach a decision *after* your presentation. By initiating and utilizing trial closes, you will pretty much know at each stage whether your prospect likes what they are hearing. In this way, you will actually be able to work together to help them buy.

A good way to trial-close is to get your prospect to rate his level of interest and commitment. For example, "Mr. Jones, on a scale from one to ten, how would you rate your level of interest right now?" If he says six or higher, you might be in the ballpark. If he says five or lower, go back and probe more. Find out if he's even qualified to buy your product. Don't waste your time by plowing through your presentation.

If your rating is below six, you might say, "Well, how would this earn a ten?" I guarantee they will be candid at this point if there is enough rapport. If they trust and like you enough, you will know on the spot what you have to do to get the business.

A technique which the great motivational speaker Zig Ziglar taught was the basic request for commitment. Zig said it this way: "Mr. Jones, do you have yourself convinced yet, or would you like to hear a little more?"

This may be a bit overt for your taste, but Zig Ziglar was brilliant. He assumed that the prospect is the only one who can convince himself. You will not be able to persuade or convince them. The idea has to come from them. He will not buy into *your* idea. He will buy his own.

Get an Overall Opinion

Another trial-close technique is to ask for the prospect's basic overall opinion of what you have said so far. For example, "Mr. Jones, based on what we've discussed so far, how does it look?"

This is a great opportunity for you to use the sight-based, the hearing-based, or the feeling-based modes we discussed earlier. If your prospect is sight-based, you might say, "Based on what we have discussed so far, how does it *look*?" If they are sound-based, you might say, "Based on what we've discussed so far, how does this *sound*?" If they are feeling-based, "Based on what we've discussed so far, how does this *feel* to you," or "How do you *feel* about it?" Using these sight-, feeling-, and hearing-based phrases will enable you to get more honest, open, and emotional statements from your prospect. This is extremely important on the phone, since it's more difficult to generate trust and rapport on the phone than face-to-face.

Probably 60 percent of a sale on the phone is made after you've probed and presented: 60 percent of your prospect's opinion is determined from how well you listened during the interview. You will frequently discover that your prospect, upon a trial close, will say, "Sounds good to me. Let's do it." Recently I said, "On a scale of one to ten, what would you rate your level of interest?" The prospect said, "Sounds great to me. I'm a ten. Let's do it." If I had not trial-closed, I probably could have talked myself out of the sale by overselling.

You'll frequently hear a prospect say, "Sounds great. Let's do it." One of the worst things you can do after this buying signal is to say, "Well, uh, uh, are you sure?" Obviously you will buy it right back. If your prospect wasn't sure, they would not say yes in the first place. By making a comment like, "Are you sure you want to do this?" or "Are you sure this is the right thing for you?" you're actually putting doubt in your prospect's mind. Often they are depending on you for the right recommendation.

Some of your prospects have developed such a high level of trust with you that they really would buy anything that you recommended. When they hear you say things like, "Are you sure you want to do this?" you've just pushed yourself out of the sale by breaking their trust.

Try to trial-close. It's a great technique, and it will allow you to find out where you are during the presentation process. Here's an example of a trial close.

KERRY: The rates on this policy, as well as the maintenance program, seem to fit with your requirements. Are lower rates still important to you?

PROSPECT: Yes, they are.

KERRY: Based on what I've presented so far, does this seem like a winner?

PROSPECT: Yes, it does. I'd like to hear more about your company's background.

Presenting Disadvantages

Would you like to learn a technique that will prove to your prospects that their well-being is your highest concern? In other words, would you like to find a technique which will actually enable your prospect to sell himself instead of you doing it? It's called *presenting disadvantages.*

I know what you're thinking: "The prospect is already thinking it won't work without me helping by telling him what's wrong." But it could really play to your advantage to let them know what's bad as well as what's good. It's natural for a prospect to mistrust the salesperson initially. They're actually trying to look for the negatives.

How many times have you been prospected by a salesperson by telephone, or even face-to-face, who told you their product was pie in the sky—the neatest thing since canned beer, mom's apple pie, and perfection all rolled up into one?

Obviously, nothing could be that good. They were trying to hype you. But have you ever heard the salesperson tell you what's wrong with a product? You probably felt taken aback, surprised, and even possibly a bit disoriented. This confusion actually helps the product sell itself.

Try sometime to give your prospect the negatives after he's already heard the positives. Let me give you an example. An insurance company in Canada named Great-West Life wanted me to speak at a convention. They asked me the topics I spoke on. I first probed the meeting planner and told her the kind of topics and the messages I gave. I presented the benefits: I was entertaining, and I presented content-filled information that would help their sales producers increase revenues. (Modest, right?)

Then I said, "But I'm really not good if all you want to do is entertain. I try as hard as I can to give salespeople transferable ideas along with the stories." I actually threw in a negative at this point. I insinuated to the planner that I wasn't her best choice if she wanted a rah-rah, hype, all-entertainment, no-content speaker. It worked like a charm. She said on the telephone, "Oh, if you can do that, it will be a great program."

Tempering my presentation with a few disadvantages brought my benefits down to earth. I became more believable and in turn pulled her to me.

The Takeaway

Earlier, I mentioned a technique called the *takeaway*. This technique can be used to let the prospect know they may not be a good candidate for your product. The same concept applies to disadvantages. You're actually saying, "This may not be right for you." All of a sudden, instead of pushing, you're actually pulling. They'll switch directions with you on the spot.

I used to own a BMW 535i, which I jokingly say is a very strange license plate for a '67 Chevy. It's one of the most gorgeous cars I had ever seen. In fact, the salesman I bought it from told me that it would beat a 911 Porsche Carrera in the quarter mile. I was pretty impressed by that. But he hard-closed me when I first saw the car on the lot. He said, "It has a wider wheel base than a BMW 635. It has better gas mileage than a Porsche Carrera. It's the kind of car that lets people know that you've arrived, but it's not for everybody."

Obviously, he did a takeaway, but he also said it was one of the best-made cars in the world. Directly after that, he said, "But, then again, some people say that the 535i has too much power. They've had a lot of traffic tickets. In fact, some say it's overpowered." He changed strategies on me. He gave me a possible disadvantage.

That made me salivate. I realized I really wanted that much power, and I really wanted that car. He told me the disadvantages that helped me buy that car.

The Twelve Worst Phrases to Use on the Phone

A good friend of mine, telemarking expert George Walther, has come up with twelve phrases that you should never use on the telephone. Avoid these when you present to your prospects. You'll prevent the prospect from becoming uncomfortable during your presentation.

1. "*Would you be interested in . . . ?*" The meaning behind this is, "Mr. Prospect, I presented a lot to you so far. You haven't been interested in anything yet. Let's try this."

2. "*To be honest with you . . .*" You're basically saying here, "You moron, I've been lying the whole time. I'm going to tell you the truth just this once."

3. "*You won't believe this, but . . .*" The prospect is thinking here, "If I won't believe it, then don't say it to me."

4. "*Could you do me a favor?*" As far as I know, favors are done by people who share fairly high rapport and are friends. When you ask a prospect to do you a favor, you're actually saying to him, "We're great friends so far, aren't we? Why don't you do

something nice for once?" Unless he's a truly good friend, I would avoid this.

5. *"Can you spell that for me?"* People often use this technique when they don't hear or understand a person's first or last name. For example, why not just be up front with that prospect? Instead of saying, "Can you spell that for me?" and having him say (embarrassingly for you), "Smith. S-M-I-T-H," say, "I didn't hear that. Please repeat that again."

6. *"I have to ask someone."* Don't say this to a prospect. If you must get higher approval, say, "My specialty is in pricing and delivery. If you want an upgrade, I would be glad to ask my supervisor about it." Be specific.

7. *"Just this once . . ."* Oh, boy. Do you really think that your prospect is going to buy the fact that he is so special that you're giving him something that you've never given anybody else? This is, frankly, garbage. Don't expect your prospects to have an IQ below room temperature. They won't buy this.

8. *"Can I get you to buy . . . ?"* This phrase says in effect, "If I push you, will you just say yes?" Have you ever known anybody who, when pushed, actually pulls back? When you push people, they don't pull back; they push back. "Can I get you to buy?" will immediately evoke *no* as an answer: "No, you can't get me to buy."

9. *"I'll try."* Don't say this on the telephone to a prospect unless you are negotiating. Either you can do it or not. Either you can

get the delivery for a prospect on Friday, or you can't. If it's really up in the air, tell you prospect exactly what the difficulties are.

10. "*Have to*," as in, "I'll *have to* ask my supervisor." Here you're really saying, "It's against my will to do this. I really don't want to. I have to."

    I was at the Dallas airport recently when a pilot came on the flight intercom and explained why we were ten minutes late. He said, "We'll have to wait here for ten minutes while some connecting baggage is loaded." If connecting baggage is loaded onto the airplane, it means that certain other passenger flights were late. The passengers got on the airplane, but their baggage hadn't yet made it. The pilot was basically saying, "If it wasn't for you idiots whose plane was late, we wouldn't have to wait for this baggage." It would have been much more elegant if that pilot had said, "Now we're going to wait for the baggage," or "We would like to wait for the baggage so that these passengers don't arrive before their clothes." Sound better?

11. "*I can't . . .*" If at all possible, you should state things in positive terms rather than negative ones. If your prospect says, "I want a 45 percent discount," don't say, "I can't get that." Say instead, "If I can get you a 30 percent discount instead, will that be OK?" Try to avoid negatives with your prospect. Work on positives. You need to project an image of trying to work on a deal rather than telling your prospect what he can't do.

12. "*What do I have to do to get your business?*" Here you are basically saying, "I'm going to coerce you against your will if it's the last thing I do." It's a lot like, "What do I have to do to get you to buy from me?"

By avoiding these twelve phrases, you'll make yourself much more appealing. Your prospect will rarely tell you specifically what you did wrong. You just have to know. Record your presentations. Play them back to your sales managers or associates. You will be able to get an idea of what you are doing wrong. But pay special attention to these twelve phrases. It may mean the difference between making a quick sale and letting that prospect procrastinate and give you multiple objections.

Twelve
Handling Objections

Have you ever received an objection from a prospect or an existing client on the telephone before? (To a salesperson, that is like having somebody come up to you and say, "Have you ever breathed before?") Receiving objections can be sheer terror, but it shouldn't be. There are excellent ways of handling objections, which will work in almost every case except for the hardest prospect.

I heard a speaker on negotiations a short time ago say to his audience, "What is the opposite of *love*?" He then asked everyone to raise their hands who responded with *hate*. Of those people who answered, he asked how many were single. Almost 85 percent raised their hands.

The correct answer is *indifference*. Indifference is much worse than hate, because if your spouse hates you, they still care, even though they're upset. Indifference shows there is really no hope for resolution. They no longer care.

This has a lot to do with getting objections from prospects. Feel lucky if you get an objection from a prospect, because it shows that they still care about your product or your service. They want to give you a chance to help solve problems and to find solutions. By giving an objection, he's saying, "I don't think this will work. Help me come up with something better."

The opposite of an objection is when your prospect says no and hangs up on you—or, worse yet, asks you to let them think about it, never intending to buy. That's indifference. If your prospect gives objections, you're still in the game.

There are three basic reasons why you get objections. Number one, the prospect is simply requesting more information. For example, if your prospect says, "It's really too expensive; I can't afford that," he could really be saying, "Please help me find a way to afford it."

The second reason for giving an objection is that your prospect is scared of buying your product or service for fear that they might be taken advantage of. They are frightened of granting an appointment over the telephone to someone they have not met face-to-face.

The third reason your prospect may give you an objection is probably the most common and the most serious. This reason will largely determine how quickly you will sell. Your prospect may give you an objection simply because you did not do a good enough job listening and probing.

The most productive and profitable salespeople in the world all know and practice the motto, "I want to help you solve your problems. I can do this because I will listen first to what your problems are."

Think about this for a second. If somebody came to you and said they want to sell you a car but didn't bother finding out anything about you before they started presenting, you likely wouldn't buy, correct?

At the same time, if that salesperson spent three or four weeks with you and then recommended a car on the basis of how well he knew your needs, you are very likely to spend the money to buy it, right? You surely would think that he's qualified to recommend a car, am I correct?

Both are extremes. You would never present without listening, but at the same time, you can't afford three or four weeks of probing, so you will always get a few objections. But these are a lot fewer than the number of objections you would get if you didn't listen at all.

The most common objection I get in my business is, "I don't want to book you just from a telephone conversation. Why don't you send me some information?" This person is saying he's first requesting more information. but secondarily saying, "I'm afraid that you may not be the person that I think you are. Let me feel more comfortable by looking at some brochures and information about you."

"Yes, But"

Now I'm going to give you some of the best objection-handling techniques ever devised. You will be able to use these to cash in and make sales from almost any objection you could ever receive on the phone.

Have you ever heard of a technique called "Yes, but"? Here's how it works. The prospect says to you over the telephone, "It's really too expensive," or "I don't buy over the telephone." Your comment would be, "*Yes*, I understand, *but* it's not too expensive. This is cheaper over the telephone than it would be on Amazon."

If it seems a little manipulative, you're absolutely right. What this "yes, but" technique does is actually push against your prospect. You're saying to your prospect, "Yes, I heard your objection, but no, you're wrong. It sounds as if you are saying, "You don't know what you're talking about. You are misinformed."

Allow Your Prospect to Be Right

Here is rule one in answering objections. Never prove your prospect wrong when they produce an objection. Always try to prove them right. You're probably thinking, "Kerry, you are nuts. If my prospect gives me an objection, I'm going to let him know the truth." Psychologically, that will always land you with a loss.

People never want to be wrong. They always want to be right. How many times have you discussed a statistic or even the weather? You know you're right, but when they find out they're wrong, they try to make up a situation allowing them to save face and be correct.

There's such an emphasis now on the avoidance of being wrong and making mistakes that we sometimes lose our willingness to take risks. Let your prospect save face. Most people in normal conversation try to find some loophole someplace in an effort to validate their own views.

I had an uncle whom I saw fairly often at family gatherings. He was probably like your uncle or any other relative who is never wrong about anything. Years ago, he and I had a conversation about communism in which he made a blatant statement: "You know, if those damn communists get out of Portugal, I think that we'd have less problems in Europe."

I didn't think there were that many communists in Portugal, and it is a NATO nation. I said to my uncle, "I don't think you're correct in that, unc." He said, "Sure I'm correct. Portugal is an Eastern European Warsaw Pact nation. It's on the east side of Bulgaria. It's overrun by communists."

As you know, Portugal is west of Spain and on the Atlantic coastline, but I decided not to argue with my uncle. I went to get an atlas, opened it up, pointed to Portugal and said, "Look, it's on the Atlantic coastline, uncle, just like I said. It's on the west side of Spain."

My uncle looked at the map, looked back at me, and said, "It must be a misprint."

Your prospect will act the same way if you try to tell the truth and they are mistaken. You will have a hard time. They will not buy from you. Prove him not wrong, but right when you hear an objection. The way to do this is to avoid changing your prospect's opinion, but instead trying to add to what your prospect already knows. If you accept this, you'll be able to overcome any objection you will ever get from a prospect from now on.

Think of dealing with your prospect in this way. He's really saying, "Based on the information you've given me, so far, the answer is no. But please give me more information tailored to my needs."

Try using this with an office mate or the next time you call a prospect on the telephone to get a face-to-face appointment. For example, tell your prospect directly after he gives you an objection how correct you think he is. Even praise him for his perceptiveness. For example, if a prospect says to you, "I just think that it won't work for me," your response from now on should be, "I understand how you would think that way. With the information I've given you so far, I'd draw the same conclusion."

If your prospect says, "I really can't afford this. It is not in my budget," your response should then be to prove your prospect correct. You might say, "At this point, it does seem too expensive, but I would like to share a couple of ideas which might make it more affordable." Prove your prospect right, not wrong.

Here is something I would like you to do: Find someone in your office. Throw objections back and forth with that individual, using the same techniques I just gave you, proving them right.

When to Answer Objections

When should you answer an objection? Before, during, after, and never.

Number one, you can answer before it is asked. This is probably the best time to answer an objection that you suspect might be coming up. If you can reply to an objection to your prospect's satisfaction during the presentation stage, you'll be much better off. The les ammunition you can give your prospect, the better.

The more quickly you can help your prospect get to the closing stage, the more effective you will be. If you do a good job presenting your product or service, you will cover most of the objections before they come up. For example, "Mr. Jones, some people have said the units on this mutual fund are price a little bit too expensive. They said that until they researched the potential for growth. Six months later they were very happy they put that much money into this fund." It's best to cover frequently asked objections ahead of time.

I once listened to a life-insurance salesperson try to get the prospect to see him on a face-to-face appointment. As he talked on the phone, he said right off the bat, "You know, Mr. Jones, a lot of people plainly don't agree with buying life insurance. They just don't think that their family is worth the trouble, but we know the low value these people put on their family in the end." This may seem heavy-handed to you, but it really slaps the prospect across the face. He will never give that objection to that same salesperson again.

The most obvious time to answer an objection is when it's asked. If the objection is a viable one, and your prospect is concerned, make it work for you by answering it. Hopefully, if you're a professional phone pro, you will work ahead of time and write down all the objections that may come up. You'll also practice them so that you'll be prepared.

If you choose to answer the objection when it's asked, get the real reason behind it. Seventy percent of the objections you get are those you will never answer to your prospect's satisfaction, because until he gives you the meaning behind the objection, you will never answer it the way he wants to hear it.

Suppose that you're trying to book a face-to-face appointment. The prospect says, "I'm sorry. I can't afford to take the time." Your response might be, "I understand you can't take the time. I promise it will be worth ten minutes. Wow, you sound insanely busy. Are you doing something that would prohibit you from hearing about this?"

Or if your prospect says, "It's too expensive. I just can't afford the money. It's not in my budget," your response might be, "I understand it's not in your budget, but out of curiosity, tell me more about your budget."

In most cases, if you ask for the real reason behind an objection, the prospect will be very straight with you. He's very likely to tell you deep down why he gave you that objection. You know as well as I do your prospect often will give you reflex objections. These are cosmetic objections designed to blow you off the telephone quickly.

Many of my clients call unsolicited to have me speak at their meetings. But like you, I also have to sell on the telephone to get the best gigs. If I send some information, I always ask for the date of the conference.

I'll say, for example, "When is your program?" They'll say, "June 15." I often do a trial close at this point and say, "I'm going to pencil this in and save it until we get a chance to talk again. Is that OK with you?" If they say "OK" or "That's fine," I'll reserve it tentatively. I know they are a qualified prospect.

The most frequent objection I get is, "We've already booked our speakers." But in my business, "We've already booked our speakers" doesn't mean a thing. When I talked to this prospect before, his program was not yet booked. What was the reason he decided not to use me as a speaker, other than that he was already booked? My job is to learn from my mistakes as well as successes.

My staff is now trained to say, "I realize you booked your speakers, but we would love to hear how you booked the other speaker besides Kerry. It will really help in our marketing." They're very likely to say, "He was too expensive. His airfare was too high. We wanted a sports figure, a celebrity to speak at this conference." Something truthful rather than just a smokescreen.

Many sales superstars use humor to break the ice before they actually answer the objection. This helps to ferret out the real objection. I once knew a telephone salesperson who said, "Is that the real reason, or are you just trying to test my sales skills?" As you can see, this probably elicits at least a chuckle from the prospect.

Another technique to get the meaning behind the objection is to say, "Gee, there must be a good reason why you brought that up. Tell me more about it." In fact, with all these techniques, you're really trying to get to the deep-down meaning behind the objection. Why did your prospect make it?

The fourth time to answer an objection is after it's made. Sometimes it's better to stall until your prospect hears more about your product or service. Sometimes it's advisable to go further into the presentation without getting bogged down in answering every objection.

Your prospect might say, "I really can't afford the interest rates in buying your product. It'll cost me too much money." If you were to stop and answer an objection like that in the middle of a presentation, you could get bogged down into answering objection after objection. Instead, you might say, "You know, that's a viable concern, and I'll get to that in just a second." Or "Good comment. You'll hear more about that in just a moment."

If you allow yourself to be sidetracked with questions during your presentation, your prospect may take control of it, causing you to lose control over the process. Be careful in answering an objection after it's asked. Often the tendency is answer right away and talk too long.

Don't forget the fifteen-second rule, which states that your prospect will lose interest if you talk more than fifteen seconds at a time—even in answering objections—especially during the presentation stage.

The last time to answer an objection is never. Have you ever had an objection that was purely foolish? It didn't deserve a response. Make sure you acknowledge it so your prospect knows that you heard it, but then ignore it and proceed with what you're talking about.

Many years ago, there was a popular TV drama called *L.A. Law.* I watched a segment. A lawyer and a disgruntled husband were negotiating over a divorce settlement. The husband, obviously upset and angry, said, "All you lawyers are snakes. Someone should take you guys and put you behind bars someplace." Had the lawyer responded to that comment (objection), not only would he have escalated the situation, he would have put validity into a ridiculous comment.

Sometimes your prospect will simply vent frustration. I once heard a prospect say, "I don't need sales training because I'm replacing all my salespeople next week with brand-new people." Gee, what a ridiculous objection. I acknowledged and then ignored it. I said, "I understand," and continued to probe more.

I didn't think his objection made any sense at all. If I had responded to it, I would have lost the sale on the spot. If you ignore an objection, which sometimes is appropriate and the prospect responds with, "You didn't hear what I said," or repeats it to you, then you must address it on the spot. Until that time, use your discretion and just move on without hesitating.

How to Get Prospects to Answer Their Own Objections

Would you like to get your prospects to answer their own objections? A technique called *playback* might help. Sometimes a prospect will answer their own objections plainly without your help.

Some very bright salespeople are able to change the prospect's own objections into ones that sound a little bit ridiculous when repeated back. If you use this the right way, you may be able to get them to tell you what they dislike about their current vendor without your ever saying anything derogatory.

For example as a financial advisor, you might hear a prospect offer an objection such as, "My broker is Merrill Lynch, and I'm very happy with him. I don't think I need another stockbroker." Doing a playback, your response is to say, "Do you mean your broker is Merrill Lynch, and you're happy with them?" Or: "I'm using Sprint, and it's working out quite well." "You're using Sprint, and it's working well?" This is a very subtle but often effective technique to get your prospect to think past his reflex responses. It might make him think, "What does this guy know that I don't know?" You may instill a sense of fear in your prospect. All of a sudden, he may doubt his current vendor. Maybe he should do more research on them.

I recently moved to a new office building in Southern California. The Southern California leasing market is extremely competitive. Commercial buildings are overbuilt, and the tenants can often negotiate a great lease price on business space. A commercial real-estate broker once called and asked me about my plans to move. I had originally decided to stay with my current landlord and go into another building, so I said, "My landlord is Loomis Properties, and I'm fairly happy with them."

The salesperson said, "You mean your landlord is Loomis, and you're happy with them?"

I felt a shudder of fear going down my back. What did this salesperson know that I didn't know? Was Loomis so poorly thought of that something might happen to me in the future? "Why?" I said. "Do you know something I don't?"

He went on to tell me how other property managers were superior to Loomis. The point is, he didn't pitch. He first grabbed my attention.

The Switch-Off Technique

The switch-off is a great way to turn an objection into a goal that you both work together to achieve. This forces your prospect to go from negative to positive. It also prohibits him from saying no. It forces him to find out how your product or service will work.

For example, he might say, "I really can't afford it." Your response could be, "I think the real question in your mind is, how would you be able to gain this solution and still be able to afford it? Is that correct?" In this way, you're looking at the outcome of buying your product and incorporating a positive spin to the objection.

For example, I hear, "We don't use outside speakers." I often say, "I think the real question in your mind is how to afford an professional speaker who really knows your industry. Is that correct?"

If at that point your prospect says, "No, that's not correct," you'd better reestablish their goals. The goal in using any speaker is to create a great program. The meeting planner wants to look good. It might be that they've never paid a speaking fee before. It might also be that they've never used an professional speaker and they're nervous about trying something new. In any event, you're pushing the prospect to turn a negative objection into a positive request for more information.

I mentioned before that I moved my business to a new location. One commercial real-estate broker was trying to present a very expensive property with more space than I needed. I said, "It's really too expensive, and it's more space than we need."

Unconsciously the broker said, "I think the real question in your mind is how you can have this much space without it being too expensive, correct?" You got it.

Seven Steps to Cashing Objections

So far I've given you tips and techniques in dealing with any objection. This next set of skills will not only incorporate some of these tips, but will also give you a seven-step approach. If you use these steps in the right way, you will rarely be stuck again in getting through an objection.

Number one, make sure you *hear your prospect out and acknowledge the objection*. It doesn't matter how many times you have heard that objection before. Listen to your prospect as if it were the first time. In a way, it truly is the first time that you have heard it in quite that way, especially on the phone. If you sound as if you receive that kind of objection all the time, you're very liable to lose credibility. If you really do hear it often, why not cover it before it's asked?

Number two, make sure you *question the objection*. Question the intent behind it. Give your prospect the chance to answer their own objection. Try letting them explain their logic behind the objection. Not only does it help you understand what is meant, but it also helps you answer more effectively later on in the way they want to hear it.

For example, your prospect might say, "It's really too expensive." You in turn would question it by saying, "Tell me more about why you feel it's too expensive."

He might say, "I don't like the location of that property."

You might say, "I'd like to hear more about why the location is bad for you."

The real benefit behind questioning the objection is simply that, again, your prospect may answer their own objection.

Through this book, I've been giving you a lot of examples of how I've been able to incorporate these techniques in my speaking and consulting business. I have sometimes realized that I oversell and get myself into trouble by answering objections too soon, without finding out more about what was in the prospect's mind prompting objections in the first place.

A short time ago, I called a prospect who said, "Your fee, Kerry, is just too expensive for our conference." I heard it out and questioned it. I said simply, "I understand that you think it's too expensive. Tell me about why you feel the fee is too high."

This prospect went on and said, "I was thinking about using you for a breakout concurrent session. Since we have four going on at the same time, I couldn't afford that much money." Then he went on to say, "We could use you as a keynote speaker. We have a separate budget for a general-session keynote speaker. I could probably use you in that slot anyway." He answered his own objection.

Here's something to remember when answering objections. If you question the intent behind the objection, your prospect will answer his own objection 50 percent of the time. Don't deprive your prospect of selling themselves.

The third step in the objection-handling process is to *prove your prospect correct*. This could very likely be used in acknowledging your prospect in the first step. Because your objective is to let your prospect know that you'd like to work for them, try to give them credit for their perceptiveness. Say something like, "I understand you feel this is too expensive. It certainly seems that way right now." Or you might say, "I know where you're coming from. It sure seems that way."

Remember when you were in grade school? There was always one student in the class who would correct the teacher's spelling. He would raise his hand in front of the class and say, "Teacher, teacher, you left the E off of *apple*." The teacher would say, "Thank you, Johnny," and she would put the E at the end of the word. (I think these kids were also the types to let the teacher know she forgot to assign homework.)

Treat these prospects in the same manner. Compliment them on catching you giving an insufficient amount of information. Praise them, and move on to answer the objection.

Number four is to *isolate the objection*. Has a prospect ever given you objection after objection? Do you enjoy that? The prospect was taking a quiver full of arrows and shooting at you. He was trying to hit the bulls-eye. When he missed, he kept shooting.

One way to stop that prospect from shooting more and more arrows at you is to isolate his most important objection from all others. Let him know you will try your hardest to answer his concerns and give more information. But at the same time, answer the objection that he thinks is the most important instead of a laundry list.

For example, your prospect might say, "It's really too expensive." The way you might isolate that objection is to say, "Is cost your biggest concern, or is there something else?" This prevents your prospect from giving you a litany of objections. Or he might say, "Well, I can't see you on an appointment next week because my brother-in-law is an insurance agent." Your response would be, "Is the fact that your brother-in-law is an insurance agent the biggest concern for not seeing me next week, or is there something else?"

Speaking of life-insurance agents, I was once told by a producer that a prospect said, "I can't afford the $1000 a month premium. It's just too expensive." The agent showed him how he could afford a bigger policy while only paying pennies more. The prospect suddenly gave another objection. "Well, my wife won't like it. She'll say no."

After the agent went over the part of the presentation that the prospect's wife might object to and what the husband could do to convince her, the prospect said, "I guess I need to think about it overnight."

This stall is the archnemesis for a producer like you. The agent had received a laundry list of objections, fighting them throughout the process. If he could have isolated the objection and said something like, "Is your wife's concerns the only reason you have right now, or is there something more important?" Anything you can do to pinpoint the real objection will help you sell on the phone.

The fifth step in the objection-handling process is to *answer in exactly the same way the prospect asks*. Use the same meaning, the same intent, and the same words your prospect used. Be creative and also use a reference sell if possible. Tell him of your other clients who have benefited, and mention names, companies and specific applications. The reference sell will even work in handling objections. But more importantly, you must use your prospect's own words if you ever hope to answer to their satisfaction.

I once talked to a VP at Connecticut Mutual Life. He wanted me to speak to his regional groups. I presented what I thought would be the best contribution to his conferences. He suddenly said, "I'm not sure that will fit. I'd like to go outside of the nine dots and ask you to give me something more appropriate."

"I understand that you think it may not fit," I said. "At this point, I wouldn't think it would fit either." I questioned it. "What's the real reason why you think it won't fit?" After I heard more, I used the prospect's own words as I answered the objection. I said, "Here's a way we can go outside the nine dots and make this fit. Would that be better?" By doing this, I accessed meaning and intent in his mind. Using your prospect's own words when communicating will be worth as much as 1000 pictures.

The sixth step in cashing and answering objections is to *confirm and get agreement*. It's imperative to get your prospect to agree or to sign off on your answer, or they may just present the same objection again.

Often after your prospect hears an answer, he will simply agree with you to save time or avoid conflict. He might say, "Yes, I understand," and then still not buy, which doesn't help you. Because of this, I recommend that you try to get him to agree that his objections were answered satisfactorily. You might say, "Did I answer that appropriately?" or "Does this seem like it may work?" or "Does that help?" It's very important to get your prospect to agree with you that there is no longer a concern. They need to let you know it was covered it appropriately.

The last step in the objection-handling process is to *do a trial close*. We discussed trial closes earlier. The best time to close, as discussed before, is right after the objection is answered. If you got the prospect to agree that the objection was answered, he may just buy from you at that very moment. If you answered it appropriately and logically, there should be no other objections. Stop the presentation and close. Say to the prospect, "Does that seem like the right way to go?" or "Should we write this up? Since I covered that to your satisfaction, should we just go ahead with it?" Trial closes should be done as often as possible.

Your prospect is most apt to buy after their objections are answered. This is the point at which you should close. We will discuss more on closing in the next section. But any time you answer an objection to your prospect's satisfaction, trial-close or you may lose a sale.

Feel-Felt-Found

One of the oldest techniques in dealing with objections is also one that's the most workable and easiest to learn. It is probably the fastest and simplest way to handle any objection. It is called the *feel-felt-found* technique.

Here's how it works. Your prospect may say something like, "It's really too expensive." Your response using the feel-felt-found technique is, "I understand how you *feel*. I've had other clients who *felt* the same way until they learned this will pay for itself in six months."

"I understand how you feel" is acknowledging the objection. "I've had other clients who have felt the same way" basically says to this prospect, "You're not the only one. You're very perceptive. You're right in having that feeling." "Until they learned that . . ." Here is where the objection is answered, which is a partial reference sell.

You get objections because the benefits and risks of your product or service are not in balance. Have you ever seen the image of the blindfolded woman holding the scales of justice? This is a very good illustration of how your prospect's mind is working. When you receive an objection, they are really saying, "So far, the risks I'm hearing are not yet outweighed by the benefits. So far, the ideas that you've given are not beneficial enough to compensate for the loss of resources." (One of those resources, of course, might be time as well as money.)

If you paid attention when I discussed how people who see, hear, and feel are experiencing and buying your product or service differently, you might have sensed the uses for the feel-felt-found technique. With sight-based people you might say, "I understand your *view*. Other clients have had the same *perspective* until they found out that . . ." For people who hear, you might say, "I *hear* what you're saying. Other clients have said that before until they found that . . ." This is a very quick, easy technique that you can use to answer objections without getting very elaborate.

The feel-felt-found technique has limitations. It doesn't question the intent behind the objection. It doesn't acknowledge your prospect or rephrase objections using their own words. It doesn't isolate objections. It doesn't confirm or get agreement, and it doesn't help you trial-close. But it could still be very effective in some situations.

The Blow-off

Have you ever received an objection early in the telephone conversation? Your prospect is trying to blow you off the telephone. Most objections you hear on the telephone will come within the first thirty seconds.

For example, "Mr. Jones, I'm calling you today because I'll be in your area on Thursday. I'd like to drop by and talk to you briefly about your copier needs."

"Why don't you just send me something in the mail? I'll call you back if I want to talk." Or you might hear, "I'm not interested. I'm too busy right now. I can't talk to you." Hearing any one of these will mean your prospect is only trying to blow you off the phone. If, for example, you say yes to sending information in the mail without properly probing and qualifying, you will waste your time.

One favorite objection technique is to say, "Just send me something." What should you do when you hear this? Should you just send the information and hope your prospect calls you back? If you do this, you'll be waiting for a long time. One technique that will work well is the Columbo approach. Columbo, in the old television series of the same name, would ask some very simple questions. As he was walking out the door, he'd ask a few more. He would take a couple more steps and ask a couple more questions—all the while giving his quarry the idea that he was on his way out. Everything was an "Oh, by the way, one last thing" kind of question. Columbo would use the question to understand, clarify, get agreement, and question again. He always tried to avoid confronting his suspect, because he wanted more information. If he pushed, the suspect would just clam up.

For example, you might say, "Mr. Jones, I'd be glad to send you our promotional brochure. You're at TJones@gmail.com, right? By the way, how many employees do you have?" You're complying with everything your prospect wanted you to do. But in addition to honoring his request for more information, you are also qualifying and probing. At this point, you can go through the whole process of approach, probe, present, and then close on the telephone.

The Reflex Response

As I stated before, you'll get some of your toughest objections in the first thirty seconds of a phone call. If you use a referral, you're less likely to get an early objection, because of your prospect's respect for the referral source. But on a cold call, your prospect will try to blow you off the telephone as fast as they can. Even with referrals, it is never a lay-down.

A mortgage-broker friend of mine is apparently on someone's financial-advisor prospecting list. He gets called at least three to five times per week. He even has a three-by-five card by the telephone offering an objection right away to the uninitiated. The card says, "Notice to stockbrokers, please say this. We have a broker. We're happy. Please don't call us back." What an objection! Even his nine-year-old son says he can usually hear a stockbroker by the way they sound on the telephone.

You'll often hear prospects say, "I don't have time to talk. I don't buy on the telephone. Send me information. If I'm interested, I'll call. I already have a broker. I never heard of you or your company before." Often these initial blow-offs are really not objections per se. They're' really negative reflex responses.

Have you ever been in a clothing store when the salesperson says, "Can I help you?" What's your immediate response? "No, I'm just looking." In fact, you will reflexively say that whether you need help or not. When someone says, "How are you?" your natural response is, "Fine."

This is also true of those of us who do business on the phone. We often say to our prospect, "I'd like to see you. I'd like to talk to you about your business. I'd like to interest you in my product." Their natural response is, "No, don't bother me. Don't talk to me. I don't have time for you."

One rule to avoid getting blown off on the telephone is, assume that your prospect has time to talk. Assume that he'll let you know if he doesn't. If he says no, then reschedule.

I've heard too many salespeople say, "Do you have time to talk?" or "Are you busy right now? Can I take a few moments of your time?" If you say this to a prospect initially, you are begging to be blown off the telephone. You're making it easy for them to say, "No, I don't have time." You've lost your opportunity. Simply assume that people are assertive. If they don't want to talk, they'll let you know.

Also, write down the ten most frequently heard objections and the answers to them. Compare those answers to those of other salespeople in your office, especially for the difficult ones, like getting blown off the telephone in the first thirty seconds. Write those out now. Then I will give you some very frequent objections that you will hear in the first few minutes; I'll also give you some answers. Please remember them, because you will definitely be able to prevent being blown off in the future.

Here are a few answers and few techniques to avoid being blown off the telephone by early objections. One is to simply humor the prospect during the first few minutes. He may say, "I never buy over the telephone." You might respond with "Well, I'm too homely to sell face-to-face."

A more reasonable technique might be the *grabber benefit*. Grabbers are those primary benefits we discussed earlier during the presentation stage. It is almost irresistible to your prospect, or should be, because you're using this to hook your prospect into staying on the telephone a little bit longer.

He might say, "I never buy over the telephone." Your response using a grabber benefit would be, "I understand you don't buy over the telephone. A lot of people don't buy over the telephone. But if I could have thirty to forty-five seconds of your time and ask a couple of questions, I might be able to save you 25 percent on your next copier."

Let me give you an example of a grabber benefit. My book *The Psychology of Productivity* was written from a request from my publisher, Jeff Krames, at Prentice Hall. He heard me speak and decided a book on sales productivity would be a good seller. Thinking about the real benefits of the book, I changed the title to *How to Increase Your Sales by 80 percent Within 8 Weeks.* (I could prove that claim.) I decided to use a grabber benefit in the title. I can't think of a single salesperson who wouldn't want this book or wouldn't at least open it up. Obviously, some people could think the title was a bit, but it sold books. The grabber benefit was rolled up in the title.

Have you ever heard, "I already have a broker," or "I already have an agent," or "I already have a cloud-based system?" If you hear any one of these things in the first few minutes of your conversation, respond by asking three questions designed to show the weakness of your competition. But only ask these questions after you praise the competitor.

For example, you might hear, "I already have VoIP phone service. I have Cox."

Your response might be, "That's a great company. I hear the clarity is excellent. Is that your experience?"

They'll probably answer by saying, "Yes, the quality is pretty good, and I've had them for a couple of years now."

At this point, you ask the three questions which you already know about your competition, which will help you uncover something they aren't currently getting. For example, you might say, "Does Cox give you their standard 20 percent discount for international calls?"

"Uh, well, no."

"If I can show you how to preserve call clarity and still save 20 percent, would you answer just a couple of questions for me?"

"Sure."

Has a prospect ever said, "I've never heard of you or your company before." In this case, let them know that this is no reason not to talk. Simply explain your company and your product.

Often you will find that prospects on the phone are very grumpy and grouchy initially. After all, your call is an intrusion on their time. How about when they say, "I'm not interested?" This is probably the toughest initial objection, because the prospect really isn't giving any information except "I don't want to talk to you." I recommend you go back and rephrase the objection. Prove the prospect correct in his assumption, and next ask him if you can ask a couple of questions.

Here's an example: "I understand that you're not interested. I wouldn't be interested either if somebody just told me a company name and expected me to respond, but would you mind if I ask a couple of questions to determine if I can save you 50 percent on your backup storage?" If he says, "No, I don't want to talk to you" a second time, move on. Don't hit your head against the wall. Don't do what some sales trainers say, "Churn and burn." You may just depress yourself. Go on to the next prospect.

But if the prospect says, "Yes, you can ask some questions," then give a grabber benefit. "I'd like to show you a way that can save 50 percent on your auto policy. Is that fair enough?" You will obviously have piqued your prospect's curiosity. He will want to hear more.

By the way, never give a grabber benefit that you can't back up. If the prospect pushed back and said, "Tell me about this 50 percent discount," and you said it was only on purchases over $20,000, you are in trouble. Hopefully, you know your market well enough.

Some prospects want discounts. Others want fast delivery, while still others want durability, low downtime, and high reliability. If you know what's most important to them and offer a grabber benefit, you'll keep them on the phone.

Sometimes your prospect is too suspicious to be cooperative with you. They're afraid of being taken advantage of. You need to make them feel very secure. If your prospect says, "I'm not interested," he's really saying, "I don't want to be taken advantage of," "You haven't given me a benefit that I like," and/or "You interrupted me."

Here's a very good technique that will help you combine a few of the things we learned as well as giving your prospect a quick grabber benefit. If she says, "I'm not interested," you might use the "I understand, and still . . . " technique by saying, "I understand you're not interested. Still, if I can just ask you a couple of questions, I may be able to save you 35 percent on your car insurance. How old is your current car?"

Did you notice what I did? I actually made a statement directly after a question. I asked if I could ask a couple of questions, and then asked a question without that person agreeing. She has two choices. Number one, she can say, "Yes, you can ask a couple of questions," or number two, she can say, "No, you can't ask me a couple of questions. I'm not going to talk to you." I don't like the second response. I'd rather she interrupt by telling me that I'm not allowed to ask any questions.

Here's another response. Your prospect might say, "I don't need life insurance." The "I understand" technique would work like this: "I understand you don't need life insurance, and still, if I could ask a couple of questions, I might be able to show you how to get a tax-free income. Do you own life insurance now?"

Try to apply this to your product. Think of the most frequently asked objections that you get. What are they? "Too expensive"? "I'm not interested"? "I don't buy on the telephone"? Your prospect could say, for example, "I don't talk to phone salespeople." Your response might be, "I understand that, and still, I might be able to save you substantial amounts of money on your next computer system. Is your system cloud-based right now or networked?" This could be a good technique when you receive an objection in the first few seconds.

Learning and utilizing these techniques will put tools in your chest. If you expect to be proficient and effective on the telephone, you need to use the right tool at the right time.

The "Why Is?" Technique

Have you ever been frustrated in answering objections? Have you ever felt nothing worked? One idea that may work is the "*why is?*" technique. It's a last resort, primarily because it's set up to pressure your prospect into looking at reality.

During the section on handling objections, I suggested that you prove your prospect right and never wrong. There are exceptions to this rule. If you are about to be blown off the telephone anyway, you'd better scramble.

The "why is?" technique tries to show that your prospect is blocking logic by being stubborn. Here's an example.

"I'm not interested."

"Why is the fact that you're not interested more important than saving $50,000 on this commercial property this year?"

In effect, you're saying, "You're giving me an objection. I understand your objection, but you're standing in your own way of getting the benefit." You're hitting him over the head with a benefit and basically telling him that he's hurting himself.

You might hear, "I already have a broker."

"Why is the fact that you already have a broker more important than getting 5 percent more than the S&P index this year?" The more negative the prospect gets, the greater the need for techniques like this.

As you can see, building your objection-handling skills will help you deal with difficult prospects. Everyone gets objections. But those objections need not be, "I don't want your product." They may be instead, "I need more information, I'm suspicious. Please help me solve my problems."

Through this chapter, I've given you three reasons why you will get objections from prospects. I've told you never to prove your prospect wrong, only right (with rare exceptions). I've also given you four general times to answer objections: before, when, after, and never. I've shown you how to do the playback technique and how to answer the prospect's questions and objections in their own words.

I've shown the switch-off technique in helping you collaborate on a goal you both can achieve. I gave you the seven-point strategy to cash objections: acknowledge your prospect, question the objection, prove the prospect right, isolate the objection, answer the objection, confirm and get agreement, and trial-close.

I've described the feel-felt-found technique. I've helped you get through early objections when prospects try to blow you off the telephone. I've shown you how to acknowledge, agree, and then go right back to answering objections.

I've told you about grabber benefits and how you can use them to keep from getting blown off the telephone initially, as well as the "I understand and still . . ." technique. We closed with the "why is?" technique.

I recommend that before you attempt any of these strategies, you should practice with an office mate or a friend. Ask them to give you objections. Then counter them by using each one of these techniques.

I'm sure now when you hear an objection, you'll be confident that you can turn it around into an opportunity In these next examples, you'll hear a few ways to deal with objections. Try to guess which techniques are being used.

KERRY: Our records show that you bought a BMW from us four years ago.

PROSPECT: Yes, it was a good car, but I own a Mercedes now, and I like it.

KERRY: You own a Mercedes, and you like it?

PROSPECT: Well, it's had a couple of problems, but it's a good family car.

KERRY: Can I ask you a couple of questions about what you like in a car?
PROSPECT: Sure, if it won't take too long.

KERRY: Mrs. Fries, my name is Kerry Johnson with Third Alert Security Systems. Hi.
MRS. FRIES: I'm not interested in security systems.
KERRY: I understand you're not interested in security systems. If I could ask you a few questions, I might be able to protect your property against the rash of burglaries in your neighborhood recently. Do you have an alarm system right now?
MRS. FRIES: No. What rash of burglaries?

KERRY: Mr. Williams, I'd like to come over next Tuesday at 3:45 to your office and discuss more about your estate to determine whether I can be a benefit to you.
MR. WILLIAMS: No, I really don't need any more life insurance right now.
KERRY: I understand you don't need any more life insurance. I think the real question in your mind as a business owner is how you can get more life insurance and pay less than you are paying right now. Is that correct?
MR. WILLIAMS: Well, I guess I could squeeze out a few moments to hear about a better deal than I have right now.

KERRY: I'd like to speak at your March conference. Do you think I would fit in?
PROSPECT: No, you're too expensive.
KERRY: I understand you think I'm too expensive. Out of curiosity, why do you mention that I'm too much?

PROSPECT: We can't afford your fee plus roundtrip New York airfare.

KERRY: Well, that's no problem, because I'll be in New Jersey the day before. Airfare will be prorated. It should only be about $300 maximum.

PROSPECT: Really?

KERRY: Does that fit better into your budget?

PROSPECT: Yes, it sure does.

Thirteen
The Art of the Close

By now, you've probably realized that closing on the telephone is much more difficult than it is face-to-face. Often, face-to-face you can actually increase your closing rate. Your prospect can see and hear you. There's a better chance of developing rapport as well as trust. It's usually harder to say no when you're face-to-face than on the telephone. Your prospect sees that you're a real person, not just a computer. He can see your eyes. He can see everything about you, reminding him you're a human being.

Unfortunately, on the telephone your prospect doesn't see these things. He doesn't see the effort you put into preparing. He only pays attention to one mode: what you sound like. Face-to-face, you will often see buying signals. She will sit forward at her desk. Her pupils may dilate.

On the phone, your prospect will show different buying signals. She'll show interest by the inflection in her voice. She will let you know when to buy by the degree to which she agrees with your ideas.

One of the great benefits of the phone is that you can close more people faster than face-to-face. You keep windshield time at a minimum. Windshield time is the amount you spend traveling from prospect to prospect. On the phone, that doesn't happen.

If you have applied these techniques, you can certainly close three or four times as many people on the phone than you ever could face-to-face.

I recently spoke to a grizzled sales pro about how he used to get people to buy. He said, "At the point I wanted a contract signed, I would take out my pen, show the gold plating, and flash it a couple times in his eyes. I would then put the pen on the table and let it roll down to the prospect, forcing him to take hold of it. At that point, he would be compelled to sign."

Techniques like this are not only manipulative but unethical. Your prospect may feel pressured to buy but may cancel the next day. There are many non-manipulative closing techniques. You'll close more easily on the phone than you ever could face-to-face and in a shorter amount of time. After you read this chapter on closing, you will be able to increase your ratio 30 percent more either on booking appointments or even buying straight over the phone. You'll close 30 percent more business just by paying attention.

One key idea on knowing how to close is instead knowing *when* to close. Your prospect should be closed at a very critical time. That is when he wants to buy.

Buying Signals

Here's something for you to think about: why not close your prospect when they want to buy instead of when you want to sell? Have you ever oversold by talking too long? Have you ever talked about things your prospect didn't care about, but you thought you had to say?

The best time to close is when your prospect want to buy, not when you want to sell. You can hear that on the phone through verbal buying signals.

These signals are responsive statements after you give key benefits. Your prospect may say, "Great. Super. Sounds wonderful." Or you may hear vocal subtleties, like his voice modulating up. A third way your prospect will give you verbal buying signals is directly after he confirms that you have properly answered an objection.

I have found the best time to close is directly after I present a key benefit matching my prospect's decision strategy. If you recall, we discussed ways that you can find out how your prospect will buy. Once you find out his buying strategy, you can present information the way he wants to hear it and close him the way he wants to be sold.

If, for example, your prospect said he previously bought life insurance because it offered protection for the family, it may still the most important reason. When you present better and newer ways of adding protection for his family, you will close. That could be the single most important thing he'll consider when buying your product.

Above all, make sure you don't oversell. If you're like me, you've probably talked too long in a presentation. Recently when all my staff people were occupied on the phone, I took a call from a gentleman requesting information on one of my audio programs. He asked me a few questions, and I probed him about his business. I then recommended which title I thought would be most appropriate to help him increase his production.

At one point, I said this: "The Peak Performance program is guaranteed to increase your sales by 80 percent within eight weeks."

He said, "Super. Sounds great to me." I went on for at least five or six more minutes, describing that it's a reward-based psychological system to help increase both activity and production by at least 80 percent within eight weeks.

He then gave me an objection. He said, "I think my activity is high enough as it is." Before, he had said, "Super and great." At that point he was ready to buy. Because I gave him more information than was necessary, I talked him right past the close.

Don't do this to yourself. Give you prospect a chance to buy when they want, not when you want to sell.

One of the best times to close is directly after you receive an objection. My guidelines on seven steps in handling objections showed you how to isolate the objection and answer it. The prospect will have absolutely no reason or excuse to say no to you. If she says, "It's too much money," you could isolate that objection by saying, "Is that your biggest concern right now?" If she says yes, and you proceed to answer the objection effectively, she will logically buy from you.

The only time you should *not* close after you answer an objection is when you get a reflex-response objection within the first thirty seconds of the initial phone call. Your prospect will give you initial objections like, "I'm too busy." "I'm not interested." "You people call me all the time. Would you please leave me alone?" This obviously is not the time to close, because you are simply trying to keep yourself from getting blown off the telephone.

After you present your product in the way your prospect wants to hear it, you may get an objection. But after you answer it, you'd better close or you will oversell yourself.

A secretary in my office violated this rule and tried to close a prospect after an initial objection. She was following up with a prospect that I had talked to a few years previously. When he said, "We really never use outside speakers," she responded by saying, "You want a great program, don't you?"

The prospect said, "Of course we want a good program."

She responded, "It's probably a good idea to use a professional speaker like Kerry Johnson. Would you like to use him for your April 17 meeting?"

The prospect said no and almost hung up.

It's inappropriate to close that quickly, because trust is not yet built up. If you already have trust and rapport, you can close during the first ten seconds. But without trust and rapport, selling is as easy as walking through a brick wall.

Another rule of thumb in closing on the phone is never to give up until you have closed. Try to close at least three times. This is a very important rule, because your prospect is often suspicious of buying on the telephone. Often your prospect doesn't trust you yet. Be persistent. Close on every call, and make sure you don't hang up until you've tried to close three times.

If you're good, you probably have a goal on every call. Whether it's to get a referral, book a second appointment, or simply sell directly on the telephone, you should know what you want ahead of time. Expect to get objections. Expect the prospect to start out negative but then gradually warm up to you.

Also expect that prospect to act like a pretty girl who says she has a boyfriend. She just keeps saying, "No, no. no. Please don't some more." She actually wants your attention and may eventually say yes, but she also appreciates your persistence. (In the Me Too era, I should add this disclaimer: I can hear in a prospect's voice a simple reflex-response objection versus a firm no. I can hear an "I'm dating someone" versus an "I'm in a committed relationship and very happy, but thanks for asking.")

Prospects are the same way. They often may want to block you to test perseverance. At a conference recently, I heard a top salesperson say it takes five contacts to get a client or to sell a prospect. Five contacts over one, two, or three years in my opinion is a bit much. I think what he was saying it will take you five contacts within a few months. But if you close at least three times on each call, it will certainly come sooner.

Another rule of the closing road is to make sure you transfer a sense of urgency. Your prospect will not buy if they can procrastinate. We discussed earlier that there are three reasons why your prospect won't buy: no need, no hurry, and no money.

You've heard of Murphy's Law, haven't you? It states that if anything can go wrong, it will go wrong. (I believe O'Toole's Law. O'Toole thought Murphy was an optimist.) The Johnson Law states that if your prospect can find a way of putting you off on a buying decision, she will.

In my business, if I let a prospect procrastinate on the telephone, there is only a 5 percent chance they will buy later. That means that 95 percent of the people that I'm not able to close right away will never buy.

Think for a second. What can you do to transfer a sense of urgency to your prospect? What can you give to buy right now? Number one is discounts. If you've ever been solicited for a magazine subscription, you probably have heard the telemarketer say, "If you buy today, I'll give you twelve units for the price of six. If you wait, you will have to pay full retail price."

You can even suggest that the prospect will lose benefits if she doesn't buy from you right now. Many salespeople say things like,

"I'll give you free delivery if you buy today. I'll give you a package deal. You'll get a discount of 20 percent."

Stockbrokers often can't negotiate the price of an investment, but they still can negotiate the illusion of a loss. A broker recently called me and said, "Dr. Johnson, you can wait until tomorrow to buy that share, but there's some interesting news that just came out today. This stock could move by 10 percent between today and tomorrow. I can't promise you that, but with the earnings report from this morning, I certainly see strength." I kept thinking how much money I would lose by not buying that stock today.

Many life-insurance agents say things like, "If I can get you to move on this quickly, I can get this through underwriting. Your policy is going to be very difficult to get through underwriting because of your heart attack. I can't make any guarantees, but there is a very good chance that a friend I know in underwriting is working today. If I call him today, there's also a good chance that I can get this placed."

One life-insurance agent in the Midwest wrote me a letter saying that he was having problems with a prospect. He couldn't get him to buy. He followed up with a phone call and tried to find out what the problem was. The prospect was still procrastinating when the agent said, "You know, last year I had a prospect who decided to wait a little bit longer, like you. He didn't think it was urgent to buy right away. During our meeting, I tried to motivate him, but he wanted to wait until the next month. The next week he had a heart attack and died in his sleep. I'm not saying, Mr. Jones, that this is going to happen to you, but I'm certainly concerned about it."

Will that work? You bet it will. It transfers urgency and motivation to him: if he doesn't do it now, he may lose something. In this case, the financial safety of his family.

Discounts are very effective. When I bought my first BMW, I test-drove the car and went home. The salesperson called me up on the phone that evening and said, "Listen, if I throw in the Bose sound system, will you buy it today?"

I often get phone calls from people who want to buy my audio programs. I often say, "I realize you did not buy the audio program during my speech last week, but I will extend the 20 percent off discount of you want to buy it now, and I will pay the postage. You will also receive a free newsletter."

The bottom line is, don't let your prospect procrastinate. Make her risk a loss of benefit if she waits. If you give your prospect a chance to procrastinate, she will. If your business is like mine, procrastinators rarely buy.

Right now you should be asking, "What is the best way to close?" In the following sections, let's talk about some very specific techniques that you can use to close more business than you've ever had before.

The Best Ways to Close

Many sales trainers say the more closes you know, the more tools you have to choose from to suit the situation. The closes I'm about to give you all fit very well into whatever situation you would like to plug them into. Some have better utility for the prospect who is difficult to deal with. Others have greater application with prospects who are already in agreement.

The most important thing is to practice these closes at least five times each to make them yours. If your close sounds contrived or canned, your prospect will know it right away.

The Assumptive Close

The *assumptive close* is built upon the idea that as you trial-close, a yes gives you tacit approval. Have you ever found a prospect on the phone who actually seemed to want to be led into making a decision? Many of your prospects don't like to make decisions. They would rather have you make the decision for them.

"Mr. Jones, we've outlined your family's needs. Do you have time next Friday for a physical?" In this way, the insurance agent assumed the sale. The idea is that if the prospect doesn't stop the salesperson, he's bought the product.

Here's another example. "Mr. Thomas, this stock issue is a real winner. I'm going to put your down for 1000 shares so we can take advantage of this. Now what is the name of your bank again?" By telling your prospect what you're doing, and then asking for the details, he very likely will go along with the flow.

I recently bought a house in Portugal with my wife, Merita. The Portuguese realtor explained how much the house was and asked if we would like to make an offer. I hemmed and hawed, and to be frank, I wasn't very committal. Then she pulled out the paperwork and asked me how to spell my first name. She went through the application, filled it out, and eventually led me to make an offer. Not only did she get an offer, I bought the house.

Nobody likes to run headlong into an oncoming train. When you do an assumptive close, you're actually saying, "I'm going to help you buy. I'm going to give you the support of preparing everything so you don't even have to make the effort to say yes. Just don't stop me."

I was closed recently by a fundraiser for a public television station this way: The phone rep explained what he wanted and probed.

He explained his need for money to keep the local station alive. When he asked me where I lived, I told him. He was familiar with my area. He said, "You live in Tustin, don't you?"

"Yes."

"With your affluent zip code, I'm going to put you down for $500 per year as a subscriber. What's your wife's name?"

"Merita," I said.

He reconfirmed my address and hung up. He didn't get a credit card. He only wanted a pledge. But it didn't mean much, since there was no contract or credit card, and I didn't even say yes. He fell a little short, but at least it was the beginning of a good close.

The idea behind the assumptive close is that your prospect will buy unless they stop you. It is probably one of the two best closes that you can ever use. It'll work in almost every situation. I use it often because I don't want the prospect to get a chance to say no.

The Minor-Agreement Close

Another close is predicated on the idea that if you can get a series of yesses, the prospect will typically buy. It's called the *minor-agreement close.* The strategy behind this is to get your prospect to make a series of small decisions. The momentum built up in making those small decisions will culminate later in a decision to buy. In other words, if you can get a prospect involved in making minor decisions, he will make a major decision later without thinking much about it. This means decision time will go down, and the number of objections will go down just as readily.

I was once closed by a international discount phone-service salesperson. He said, "You probably want a free calling card for making these phone calls when traveling outside the U.S., right?"

"Yes. I want that," I said.

"Oh, by the way, you also want a 35 percent discount during the day, correct? With an extra 45 percent at night beyond the 35 percent discount. Is that right?"

"Yes," I said.

"OK, you'll be hooked up by Friday." This phone producer had initially probed regarding my telephone usage. But when he started presenting, he bypassed the stage of telling me about costs and immediately asked me questions leading up to the sale.

To be honest, I did give this guy an objection. I said, "Wait a minute. Not so fast. Tell me more about your company." He could have just as readily presented the company and then asked me a series of minor questions to grab my interest. Nonetheless, the minor-agreement close is extremely effective.

Once a travel agent was trying to sell me a Mediterranean cruise over the telephone. She said, "You want to go to Europe this summer, correct?" I said, "Yes." She said, "How much are you prepared to spend?"

"Oh, about $4000," I said.

"She said. "Where would you like to go?"

I gave her an itinerary of the different locations I wanted to visit. She said, "Do you want to stay at the Savoy in London on the way to the cruise?"

I gave her an objection. I said, "That's a little too expensive for my taste. What else do you have?"

Not all small agreements will end up in a sale for you. These agreements must be things that your prospect will typically say yes to, not major decisions. For example, my financial planner once said in selling an investment over the telephone, "Kerry, you want high growth, right?"

I said, "Of course."

"You want a 9 percent return," he said.

"You got it."

"You also want quarterly dividends, don't you?"

"Yes."

"Let's get you under this XYZ fund." When he said, "I'm going to put $10,000 in this," I bought from him on the spot.

The Upsell

Have you ever noticed that the best time to close is directly after a prospect has already bought? Your toughest job is to get the prospect to say yes and make a decision the first time. After she does, getting her to buy something else is child's play. If you have more than one product, why sell just one? Why not sell both or all to the same prospect? She is most receptive after having just purchased. After she buys, don't be afraid of overselling with an add-on. For example, if she's just bought a life-insurance policy, you might talk next about disability. If she's just bought a stock or bond over the telephone, you might quickly discuss an alternative investment directly afterward.

Have you noticed immediately after you book a hotel room, such as Hilton or Marriott, they'll ask you right away if you need a rental car? Your airline will display a pop-up ad asking you if you need a car rental when you get there. Recognize the upsell?

It's often difficult to get people to buy initially. It's easier to get them to make a follow-up buying decision. Let me give you an example. Recently a financial company in Wisconsin asked me to speak at their conference. When they found out my fee, the program chairman agreed and said, "Can you speak on Saturday morning at 9:00?"

When we consummated the deal, I told the program chairman I would send the agreement. But before I got off the telephone, I said, "By the way, your group also has a spouse's meeting. Is that true?" She said, "Yes, we do have a spouse's event." I said, "Why not let me do another program on stress for the spouses later on that day? Do you have plans so far for them?"

She said, "Well, we were going to take them shopping, but your idea is pretty good." I said, "I'm going to be there anyway. You would certainly save on airfare." She said, "Sounds good to me. Let's do it." In that way, I made double my speaking fee just by following up and suggesting another service. If you have another service available, why not sell it? Right after a purchase is the best time for them to buy another.

The Alternative-Choice Close

In my opinion, the two best closes to use are, number one, the assumptive, and, number two, the alternative-choice close. The latter is extremely effective, because your prospects tend to focus directly on the question asked. They also tend to keep very few options and alternatives in their minds at once. They tend to respond better to limited choices. Those choices are, basically, should I buy, or should I not? Should I see that person on a face-to-face appointment or not? Should I buy one or two?

This is an important facet of human behavior. We really crave simple choices. Give your prospect a simple choice as part of a close.

When my daughter Stacey was two years old, she wanted to play with things she was not allowed to touch. One day she grabbed an expensive vase. When I tried to take it out of her hand, she screamed and yelled. Being the indulgent father that I am, I tried to please

Stacey as much as possible. I decided to use an alternative-choice close. I said, "Would you like a doll or a game to play with?" I sidetracked Stacey enough that she said she wanted the doll and gave me the vase.

You can't totally change the subject with your prospect, but you certainly can alternate choices. Instead of offering your prospect a yes answer, why not instead ask if they want 1000 units or 1500 units to start? "Is $45,000 or $50,000 of whole-life insurance more attractive right now, Mr. Prospect?" You can even use this technique with appointments. "Should we meet Tuesday at 4:15 or Wednesday at 5:45?"

One important thing to remember is that you should *not* try to mix choices or benefits together. The whole idea of the alternative choice is to be simplistic. If you complicate it by mixing choices or benefits, it will lose its effect, and your prospect will become confused. One way of mixing is to say, for example, "Mr. Jones, can we meet Tuesday at 4:45 at your office or Wednesday at 5:45 at Mimi's Restaurant?" The alternative-choice technique works well if you keep your prospect focused on two choices. Don't complicate things by giving more choices than necessary. This also helps block objections.

I recently bought tennis rackets online. After reading *Tennis Magazine*, I called a number in the magazine and asked the lady how much the rackets were. She said, "$149." I said, "I'll get back to you after I talk to my wife."

The lady wisely understood that if she lost me on the telephone, I would never buy. She said, "We're almost out of these tennis rackets. The manufacturer has discontinued the line. We only have a few left. Which would you like, three or four rackets?"

I bought four. She turned me from a prospect who was moderately interested to a proud owner of four new Babolat tennis rackets.

The Compromise Close

Have you ever been close to making a sale, but to your surprise the prospect gave you an objection such as "I need to talk to my accountant," or "I need to talk to my wife"? Sometimes when your prospect is on the threshold of buying, they can be prompted to yes by a very effective negotiation technique called the *compromise close.*

Here's how it works: Rather than trying to get your prospect to buy everything, compromise a little bit. Don't expect as much from your prospect. Get him to make a smaller investment at first.

The way to compromise-close is to try to close the normal way. If you get an objection you can't handle, try to reestablish agreement with what your prospect wants. Try to say instead, "I think you mentioned buying an alternative investment this month, correct?" Make sure you reaffirm that you know your prospect's goal. Then compromise by getting him to make a smaller initial investment. Say, for example, "Mr. Jones, I understand you need to run this by your accountant, but do you agree that this seems like a good investment generally and fits your financial objectives?"

"Well, I guess I do, but I still need to run this by my accountant."

"Mr. Jones, rather than lose this opportunity, let's make a partial investment of only 1000 shares rather than the initial 5000 we talked about."

The premise is, if your prospect stalls, they will procrastinate and never buy. Instead, get them to agree to a lesser sale. This is especially important on the telephone. If you're selling paper clips and trying to push that prospect to buy 10,000 boxes, decrease it to 5000 to avoid the stall.

Negotiators use compromises frequently. They try to make a negotiation a win-win situation as often as possible. They frequently can't always have everything they want, but at the same time, they get most of what they want. Salespeople should act and react the same way.

The Recommend Close

Have you ever noticed that physicians have almost a 100 percent closing rate? (I bet you never thought physicians were salespeople, did you?) You'll spend hundreds or even thousands of dollars just getting their advice, largely because of the amount of respect they engender. The attitude you have probably is, "He's a doctor. He should know," but doctors are very often wrong. Their advice is faulty. That is why we are encouraged to get second opinions, especially in complex cases.

One reason why we so freely accept the advice of physicians is that they use a technique called the *recommend close*. It works like this: "Mr. Jones, based on what I have heard so far about your requirements for durability and your budget constraints, I recommend our new 335 copier. It will give you the specifications you require as well as still fitting within your budget. Does this seem like the right way to go?"

I once was called by a magazine telemarketer who said, "Dr. Johnson, based on your interest in tennis and world events, I recommend *Tennis World* magazine and also *Newsweek*." This close works well because of listening. If you do not probe well, you cannot use the recommend close, but if you do probe effectively, your prospect will immediately assume that you listened. You presented your professional opinion and advice in recommending a product or service that would be a solution to their needs.

The reason this close works for physicians is that they diagnosed you effectively. You put your trust in them and their diagnosis because they took a long time finding out what your problem was. When they recommended something, you took their advice.

The recommend is my favorite close. It's more effective for me than the assumptive or alternative-choice close. I like to listen and probe my prospects well. I don't let prospects ramble. But when I hear enough, I will stop the prospect and say, "I understand that you want more production, more incentives, and more productivity. That's why I recommend . . ."

I suppose one reason this works so well for me is that I let the prospect know I listened well and know his goals. I repeat their goals during the presentation stage. Then I simply say, "I recommend you take this course of action." Unless they are more of an expert than I am, they will typically do what I recommend.

Time Wasters

Have you ever had a prospect on the phone who seemed to waste your time? Me too. You called a few times, and you just couldn't get them to commit. I know this happens in my business. We have prospects off and on the phone, sometimes for two or three years. They never seem to commit to using my services.

We have a rule in my office: "Either close it or forget it." We want to follow up with prospects and give them a chance to buy eventually, but just like in your business, 20 percent of the people we contact give us 80 percent of our revenues.

Try to clear out prospects who are wasting your time. Our files show that we often talk to prospects at least once every six months.

Certainly we don't want to follow up weekly, or even once a month, but often we communicate with them five to ten times without their ever saying yes.

Would you like to find a technique either to push your prospect to say yes or to clear them off your list to make room for another qualified prospect? Here's a sentence you might consider: "Mr. Jones, we talked a couple of times now about this donation to the Child Security Fund. I really need a yes or no right now as to whether you want to help us solve these problems."

It's best, as you see, to attach a strong benefit to the end of the statement. There's always that chance you may be able to shock your prospect into a yes by letting them know that you're not going to spend any more time.

Obviously, this is also a bit of a last-resort close, but isn't a no is better than no response at all? Remember the difference between love and hate? It's much better to get a negative from your prospect than uninterest.

I once worked with a group of stockbrokers and frankly told them to look at their files and clear out all those prospects who had not made a purchase in the previous year. Stockbrokers often do a very good job of following up, but sometimes they spend too much time trying to sell prospects who are unlikely to buy anything. It's very difficult to clear out clients with whom you have a good rapport, but we pushed those stockbrokers into making this one statement: "Mr. Jones, our records show that you have not made a transaction in the last nine months. Would you mind if I tossed your file away?"

You know what happened? A full 50 percent said, "Please, don't throw my file away." They then made a purchase. They felt so uneasy about having their file erased that they struggled to maintain the relationship by buying something.

You might want to consider this with prospects you're not getting through to. Realize that there is a certain amount of follow-up that needs to be done, but some prospects may simply waste your time. Say to that next person, "I'm going to cut my losses and work with somebody else. Either buy or get out." Pretty tough statement, but you'll be surprised at the results.

The Pause Close

Another close is called the *pause close*. Sometimes a prospect who is uncomfortable with silence will actually let you make use of that silence. Sometimes they will be so uncomfortable with silence that they will try to fill the void.

You can say, for example, "You can get a 20 percent discount and free delivery," then pause directly afterward. You will make that prospect sufficiently uncomfortable that it will elicit a response. The downside is they may say no, but they're very likely to say yes. If you are uncomfortable with silence as well, you can just ask for their opinion. One good way is to say, "What are your thoughts?"

Some of your prospects are good negotiators. When they sense close, an opportunity might come to get more concessions out of you. Some concessions might be to get a lower price or get extra benefits. Sometimes, as in the case of buying consumer goods like TVs, stereos, and video players, they'll ask for your best offer. Then go to your competitor and say, "Look what he's giving me. Can you beat this?"

Have you ever heard, "I'd like to buy this, but first can you give me a 10 percent discount? You can? Great. I'll give the information to my wife."

Your job is to turn the request for compromise into a closing opportunity. Instead of offering a 10 percent discount, you should say, "Mr. Jones, if I can give a 10 percent discount, can we get this done today?" "If I could give you free delivery, would you make your purchase today?" "Mr. Jones, if I could save you $300 on airfare, can we get an agreement signed right now?"

If your prospect says no, the obvious response would be, "My goal, Mr. Jones, is to provide solutions to hit your goals. Do you think we have done that?" Your objective in this case is not to let your prospect work you and then procrastinate or go to somebody else to get a better deal.

Appointment Closes

So far, I've talked about general closing techniques. I've discussed both closing a prospect and trying to book a face-to-face appointment. But now let's get more specific.

Appointments are often as difficult to gain on the telephone as a purchase. The best closes in gaining an appointment are the assumptive, alternative-choice, and recommend closes. You may even wish to use a combination of these when booking appointments face-to-face.

When I first started selling myself as a speaker at the ripe old age of twenty-six, I made cold calls from a directory called Contacts Influential. This listed businesses by industry. For example, it listed all the real-estate companies within a given location as well as insurance agencies and even accounting firms.

I was taught by a colleague of mine to start using the alternative-choice close. After I explained who I was, I said, "Hi, Mr. Jones, my name is Kerry Johnson. I want to talk to you about helping your salespeople increase production. I'd like to see you next Tuesday at 3:30, or is 4:00 better?"

Most prospects would say, "No, I'm not interested." One prospect, after three calls said, "Boy, I know what you're trying to do to me. I'm a salesman too." He obviously thought that I was being manipulative. He knew I was new and was closing much too hard and inappropriately. I neglected to get rapport on the cold call, ask questions, and probe. Most importantly, I needed to present a couple of grabber benefits in an effort to book an appointment face-to-face.

One rule I've always had is never allow your prospect to call you back regarding an appointment. You'll never get it. If you get them on the phone, don't allow them to say to you, "I'll have to check my schedule and call you back," or "I'll have my assistant call you back regarding when I'm free." They will never call. You'll never get that appointment. Instead, make a tentative appointment time. "Mr. Jones, I realize you don't have your calendar in front of you right now. But just for now, how about Thursday at 4:00 until you get a chance to get back to me?" Better? You bet.

The best way to get an appointment is to develop high rapport. If you have rapport, good things will come to you. If you do not have rapport, you will not possess the currency of interpersonal relationships. If your prospect senses that you care, closing will be much easier. They can sense either manipulation or a sincere desire to help. Low-rapport salespeople close about 1 percent. High-rapport salespeople often find their closing rate is more than 20 percent on the phone.

The best example of manipulation is how lions hunt. You probably know that the breadwinner is the lioness, not the male. She's the one that hunts the prey, kills it, and brings it back to the pride.

Male lions sleep all day and protect their status from other males. (What a great life they have, huh?) There are always gazelles nearby, which the lions prey on. If the wind is with them, smell alone will not prompt the gazelles to flee. When the lion family is fed, they will lie around and sometimes even walk calmly. When the lion family grows hungry, and the lioness decides it's her time to hunt, even a flick of her eyebrow or a slight ruffle of her fur will send the gazelles scurrying. It's not just the chase that causes fear in the gazelles. It's the look of the lioness, the behavior of the predator. It's the message the lioness gives by very slight verbal and nonverbal cues to let the gazelles know she is hunting. She is not just hanging around.

This is the same connection that you have with your prospect. Your prospect is the gazelle. You are the lioness. If you look like a predator, your prospect will feel hunted and will not buy from you.

It's very difficult to probe when you have no trust. On the other hand, if you appear to want to help your prospect rather than taking something, he will work with you in getting what you want.

In this chapter, you learned many techniques for getting your prospect to buy on the phone. You learned that closing is harder on the phone than face-to-face, because you aren't able to see the nonverbal cues and nuances your prospect gives. You also found that the best time to close is when your prospect gives you a verbal or a nonverbal buying signal: they will modulate their voice or use buying phrases to let you know they are interested. These include, "When can I get it?" or "Does this include taxes?"

You've also learned to close your prospect at least three times before you give up. You should transfer a sense of urgency. You should let your prospect know that if he waits, he will lose a benefit. You've also learned the assumptive close, where you actually lead your prospect through a buying sequence so gracefully that he doesn't say no.

You've learned the minor-agreement close. You've learned to ask questions that require very little thought and little commitment in an effort to progress through the sales process.

You learned the upsell close: once your prospect buys one product, he is very likely to buy an add-on as well. You learned the alternative-choice close, which gives your prospect two simple choices to pick from, obviously heavily weighted in your favor.

The compromise close was discussed also. That kept you from losing a prospect about to buy by simply dropping the number of units, helping your prospect say yes to a lesser amount.

The recommend close is a very successful technique, but you will have to probe extremely well before you can use it.

The yes-or-no close is for those you're about to give up on. They've not done business with you, and you need to weed them out as contacts.

With the pause close, once you ask a closing question, you need to create sufficient tension in your prospect so they will answer in the affirmative.

The "if I could, would you?" close allows you to keep your prospect from nibbling for extra benefits and then still not following through with the sale.

In the appointment close, you've learned how to use a combination of assumptive, alternative-choice, and recommend closes in an effort to book an appointment face-to-face.

You've learned to keep high rapport and maximize the amount of trust between you and your prospect. You've also learned to make sure that you probe first and present a couple of grabber benefits before you ask that prospect for an appointment.

Using these techniques will undoubtedly help you sell more effectively. This is part of the overall sequence of gaining business on the telephone. In other words, help your prospect make decisions, and allow your prospect to buy more quickly.

Here are some examples of the closes I mentioned. Try to determine which you like best.

KERRY: Dennis, the stock issue that we've been talking about looks very good. You mentioned earlier that $100,000 wouldn't be a problem for investments you like.

DENNIS: Well, yes, I could if I wanted to.

KERRY: I believe this is the one. If you sign the paperwork today, I can get this done by the end of the day. Let me write down your address first to start the account.

KERRY: So far, Bob, you've mentioned that you want investments that have medium security with a 10 percent minimum growth. You also would like tax benefits, right?

BOB: Yes, that's what it looks like.

KERRY: I recommend Whitehall Capital fund because of your investment perspective. It'll achieve your goals easily.

BOB: Well, I'd like to think about it. Can you send me a brochure in the mail?

KERRY: I understand you'd like to wait, Bob, but what is your biggest concern about waiting longer?

BOB: I guess I don't want to lose money.

KERRY: If I could show you their track record over the last ten years, would that help?

BOB: Sure, if they have good historical returns, I'd probably do it.

PROSPECT: I want the streaming audio player thrown in on the Cadillac deal for free.

KERRY: If I could get you the player, would you come down right now and do the paperwork?

PROSPECT: Well, I'd really like to know if you'll throw the stereo in first.

KERRY: I'll work it out. Would you like the eight-inch display or the eight-inch?

PROSPECT: The eight-inch.

Fourteen
Dealing with Difficult Customers

Have you ever dealt with a difficult client or customer before? How about one you were unable to contact a second time or went radio-silent?

In the first and second year of my consulting practice, I would often schedule a speech. But when we sent the agreement to the client, it would never be returned. This was very frustrating. Since nothing was laid in concrete until the agreement was returned, we usually didn't know whether I would be stood up at the altar.

More commonly, prospects don't return calls. Perhaps you've had difficulty in the past getting through to a decision maker, even though you've had a strong referral.

Through this chapter, I'm going to give you a few steps that will help you solve some of these problems more effectively. I'll show you ways not only to get your prospect or customer to call back but to help you reconnect with them. Getting them to respond faster will save you valuable time.

Here are a few steps guaranteed to get your prospects to call back faster. Make sure your voice-mail message is specific. Make sure your message is direct and to the point. In the past you might have said, "This is John Jones; please call me back." Chances are if you leave it at that, your message will be at the bottom of twelve or fifteen other messages left before yours. If he gets back to you at all, it will be in ten or fifteen days.

Instead, leave your name and your phone number (twice, of course), and say, "Mr. Smith, this is John Jones. My phone number is 379-4223. Please call me back regarding Neil Thomas." Or to an assistant, "Please tell Mr. Smith that John Jones called regarding his IRA or his CD."

I can't stress enough how important it is to let that prospect know exactly what your call is about in order to get a callback. Often that prospect will call back to see if there's been a mix-up. He may call to tell you that he doesn't have an IRA or a CD and that you must have mixed him up with somebody else.

If you have the strength of a referral and you leave a voice mail saying, "Mr. Smith this is John Jones calling regarding Neil Thomas," he may call you back to see if there's something wrong with his friend. Out of courtesy, prospects will call back more quickly if you leave a referral's name in the message than when you leave no name.

The rule here is the more specific your telephone message, the more likely it will be returned. The less specific, the longer it will take, if it is returned at all.

What if you don't have a referral name to leave and still want the prospect to call back? As I said earlier, many sales trainers recommend that you never leave your name. They're afraid that once the prospect finds out that you are selling security alarms, they'll hang up before you ever get a chance to speak to them.

I disagree. I think that if you are telemarketing, you should make every effort to get that prospect to call back. Even if you're making hundreds of calls a day, a large number of prospects will call back if you leave the right kind of message.

If you don't feel comfortable leaving a message, at least let that person know that you called. If they recognize your name as someone who called before, they will be more apt to take your call. Leave a message like this: "Mr. Smith, this is John Dance from San Diego calling. I'll call back again." Or you might say, "Mr. Jones, this is John Thompson from Xerox Corporation. I'll call back tomorrow."

The psychology is important. We are more willing to engage with people if we've heard of them before. If you leave a message, you're actually advertising your name, ensuring a higher chance of probability of getting through the second time.

Let me give you an example. Many years ago, I read in *Newsweek* many years ago about a young comedian named Jay Leno who played a lot of clubs in the U.S. A week or two before New Year's Eve, I saw his name again, advertised in a newspaper in Orange County, California. He was going to be the headliner during a New Year's Eve show. I called up Ticketron and made reservations for my wife and me. Had I not read that brief paragraph in *Newsweek* about him, I might have thought of him as no different from any other comic on the face of the earth.

The same thing applies when leaving your name. Leaving a voice-mail message is plainly good PR. You may even encounter am assistant who says, "Oh, yes, Mr. Smith. I remember talking with you yesterday. Let me see if I can page him for you." In other words, even the secretary who has heard your name before realizes that you tried to call a day earlier. She may be more willing to help you get through on a second attempt.

The second rule for getting your prospect to call back is to arrange a telephone appointment. If you know you're going to be on the phone making a dozen calls or are trying to get through to a busy prospect, make an appointment for them to call you before 5:00 on Wednesday, or between 3:00 and 5:00 today.

Have you noticed that when people have called you and left a message with a very specific time in which you can reach them, you will be more likely to return the call during that window period? The same thing holds true for your prospect. If you offer an available time period to call you back, you will improve your chances of a callback. The one caveat is that if you make the appointment more than one day away, they will forget.

Frequently I leave messages for prospects saying, "Please call me before 12:00 noon. I'll be gone for the rest of the day." Or "Please call me back on Friday. I'll be gone all next week."

The best method for getting a telephone response is, "Please call me back between 11:00 a.m. and 12:00 noon. I'll be free to talk to him at that time." You will be more likely to get a callback.

Do you have a prospect or client who knows you, yet won't call you back? Do you have a prospect who is in the sales process, but whom you can't seem to reach now? If you're like me, you've talked with at least a few prospects who initially seemed very interested; you even sent written correspondence outlining your ideas, products, and services. But problems arise when you try to follow up. They don't return your phone calls, because they think they already know what you're calling about. Their rationale is that they doesn't have a firm answer for you yet, and that they have things more pressing than talking to you. Also, as previously noted, we forget 70 percent of what we hear in one day and 90 percent of what we hear in three days. Chances are, they can barely remember who you are. But even if they called back and said, "I don't have any information yet," it would be better than no phone call.

I have a great tip for you. If you've already sent a letter or an email, you probably have a copy. Forward your last email to them regarding your past conversations and when they should call you back. I often do this when I haven't been able to reach prospects by phone. I remind them of previous conversations from the content of the email.

Making a phone call is a good use of time. Unfortunately, if you have to call your prospect four or five times, it becomes a waste of time. But forwarding a past email is a great way of helping your prospect remember what you are both working on.

The straight truth is that some prospects just don't respond to the phone as readily as others. They don't call back as quickly, because phone contacts may be a low priority for them or because they just don't think they have any useful information for you. Even though it would take longer for them to write an email to you than to discuss the subject on the phone, they will often dictate an email instead.

Let me give you an example. I contacted a company called Lowry Financial. This successful broker/dealer company, well known within the financial-services industry, had a vice president who previously had asked me to speak at his annual convention. I called him to confirm his decision to use me as his speaker, as well as the date for his convention. He wasn't in, so I called back a second, third, and fourth time.

Finally frustrated, I forwarded a previous email. I also wrote, "John, I don't know if you've been getting my phone calls, but I'm simply trying to firm up our date in June for this conference. I want to find out more about the people attending it." I didn't call him back again.

He wrote back one week later responding to the note and stating, "We're still looking forward to having you. Sorry I've been delayed in getting back to you. I'll call you back Tuesday to firm this up." That simple piece of information worked wonders in helping our sales process, because even his telling me he had no information was better than silence. When you use this technique, you'll find 50 to 75 percent of your prospects who won't return your phone calls will return a personalized, forwarded past email. As a last resort, we frequently write an email requesting a simple yes or no decision.

Generally, I encourage my staff never to call a prospect more than three times. We are mindful of spending too much time on the telephone trying to get through to prospects who will never call back. Often, after we've made four or five phone calls, a negative prospect will simply have a staffer call back and say, "Mr. Jones is not interested." This is not what we want to hear. We don't want to bug or harass our prospects, but we do want to conduct business in a professional way.

Prospects who have been difficult to communicate with are often afraid of permanently losing contact with us. Several years ago, I finally got through to a negative prospect. "Mr. Jones, I've been trying to contact you for a few months now to find out more about how I can contribute to increasing the effectiveness of your sales force."

He said, "I really don't have a need for you right now, but I'll call you in the future."

Frustrated after being put off for so long, I said, "Mr. Jones, would you like not to be contacted anymore?" After a moment, a shocking thing happened. He said, "Of course not. I want to stay in contact with you. It's just that now is not the right time. Don't lose touch. We should keep in contact."

Right then and there, I recognized a way of molding prospects to be more positive. This executive didn't really want to lose touch. He wanted to keep in contact.

So s a last resort, you may wish to say to your prospect, "Look, I've tried to cooperate with your needs. Would you rather not be contacted anymore?" You may be able to move some prospects off the block and into your court.

When Customers Complain

Have you ever had a customer who was unhappy with your product or service? I recently saw a cute cartoon in a newspaper about a customer at a complaint window. The worker at the window was saying, "Now let me get this straight. You mean if I kill myself, bomb the store, and then bankrupt our corporation, you'll be happy?" Obviously, some customers are very vocal in their complaints.

New research shows there is a very low percentage of dissatisfied customers who will ever complain. They won't give you a chance to rectify the situation. Indeed studies conducted by the Technical Assistance Research organization show that 95 percent of your unhappy customers will never complain. They'll simply discontinue buying from you and will sabotage your marketing with bad reviews. Then these unhappy customers will tell ten to twelve other people about their experiences. These ten to twelve people will tell approximately ten to twelve other people about you. Statistics show that 13 percent of unhappy customers will tell more than twenty other people about you. Loyalty goes out the window, and your marketing investment is undermined.

Here's a prime example of negative word-of-mouth advertising. Northwest and Republic Airlines merged in October 1986. While it was a very good airline, Northwest made a critical mistake. Because of merger and computer problems, they would often experience two-hour delays for six months after the merger.

I was in Boston during that time, sitting in an airplane fully loaded. We spent ninety minutes on the ground before departure, waiting for a truck to come to help the plane start its engine. Ninety minutes on the ground for a truck! Once it arrived and started the plane's engines, we spent another hour on the ground while they looked for a tug to push the jet onto the runway. All in all, we spent more than three hours sitting on the ground waiting. Northwest made almost every customer on that flight unhappy. Conceivably more than 2000 to 3000 people had a bad taste in their mouth about Northwest Airlines. I didn't fly that airline again until Delta bought it twenty years later.

Here's the good news, though. Customers who complain are six times more likely to buy from you again if they can talk to you about their bad experiences. How do you reclaim those customers who have been dissatisfied with your product or service? Rather than avoiding those who had unfavorable opinions, search them out. Make an effort to mend fences.

One way of keeping dissatisfied customers from ruining your marketing effort is to call all past customers. They'll often be impressed by your follow-up. This will create referrals. If you keep in touch, you will have in effect bought a salesperson for nothing.

For example, I recently spoke to an interior-design conference. One woman out of the 300 in the room stood up in the front row and walked out of my program. This is not the kind of thing I like to have at my presentations. Since this was very distracting to the rest of the group, I decided to go with the flow. I said over the microphone, "Ma'am, ma'am." When she turned around, I said, "I didn't leave when *you* came in."

This is usually very humorous, but at this particular conference at that moment, nobody laughed. I was devastated. I hurt my chances of doing other programs in that industry. Attendees would talk about me negatively to other groups after the presentation. Bad word of mouth often grows more quickly than positive word of mouth.

When I called the regional director for this association nine months later, he told me how much he disliked my program and how inappropriate I was in telling that woman not to leave. I apologized for my remark and listened to him make his complaints and comments. We talked for about ten more minutes. He turned into a fan of mine and gave me more business.

You would not expect that from somebody who seemed negative about your product or service. But those who are the most vocally critical of you are often the ones most easily turned around. The more quickly you can get to disgruntled, disheartened customers, the more loyal they will be with you in the end.

Stay in Touch with Customers

Do you have repeat customers? Do you fully appreciate how much these folks save you in marketing costs? If you've ever lost a good customer, you quickly appreciate the rest of your customers.

According to current research, 68 percent of the customers who stop doing business with you or decreased their business do so because of the perception that you don't care. The University of Virginia evaluated how professionals keep their customers. The researchers examined such factors as technical expertise in their industry and price of the service, as well as intangibles like rapport. The study concluded, hands down, that customers stay with their CPA or lawyer or doctor by virtue of the rapport they have established. Rapport was the single most important factor in retaining customers and clients.

How do you keep rapport with a customer or client? One top-notch method is to maintain frequent contact. A newsletter is a way of keeping in contact. Unfortunately, it is very impersonal. A phone call, of course, is best.

The life-insurance industry is known for training its salespeople extremely well. Agents usually have 500 to 1000 clients they rarely communicate with. A company specializing in replacement of insurance policies, Primerica goes after the customers' policies, replacing them with a term policy. Often this term policy is more expensive than the policy that was replaced.

One reason that Primerica is able to make such inroads is that the agent who initially sold the product has lost touch. They have neglected the client and lost rapport. The client initially bought because of rapport. But by keeping in touch, you will cause clients to do more business and give you referrals like a water spigot. All you do is call and turn on the referral generator while selling new business.

I recently called one of my clients at the Utah Association of Independent Insurance Agents just to say hello. I was connecting through the Salt Lake City airport. Because I called to see how things were going, the client booked me for another program. Some calls that are made simply to say hello turn out to be the most beneficial.

You will spend the greatest amount of time and money developing new clients. You will expend the least amount of money and time for the bigger revenue that comes from existing clients. From now on, call them on a scheduled basis. When they recognize that you care, they'll stay with you. They'll call you before they even consider replacing your product.

A number of years ago, there were two gentlemen who kept in contact because of their friendship. One was marketing consultant Regis McKenna, and the other was Don Valentine. Regis decided to call Don Valentine to say hello. As they discussed family and their private lives, they gradually moved the conversation to a company that Regis thought Don might like to investigate. That telephone conversation gave birth to the first financial backers of Apple. That personal phone call led to the seed financing of the most highly capitalized company in the world.

Keep in contact with past clients. They will give you more business and cost you less money to secure than new ones.

Fifteen
Hiring the Perfect Telemarketer

Have you ever searched for the perfect person to hire? Whether that person is just trying to make appointments on the telephone or is selling only on the phone, they will have to overcome some challenging obstacles. You could help them by knowing how to pick the right people, the ones with the highest chances for success.

That candidate's psychological profile reads like one for a prison guard. They must be able to take rejection and psychological abuse, detach themselves from negative people, and most importantly, be persistent and tenacious. They have to be patient in almost any situation they're in. They must also be able to read prospects or clients like a book without ever seeing them. Tough order.

Very few people exist with those characteristics. When you couple the difficulty of finding the right person who can handle the enormous amount of psychological abuse and rejection that comes with the job, it becomes a one-in-a-million shot to ever find the right person.

Your phone salespeople will take more psychological abuse in one hour than a face-to-face salesperson could encounter in an entire week. This is one reason why candidates must be naturally enthusiastic as well as assertive. If your new hire does not have these psychological characteristics, you will simply add to the nationwide statistics of telephone salespeople who didn't make it.

Wall Street statistics show that stockbrokers have one of the highest attrition rates in the country. Over 95 percent will quit or be fired within three years. I should know; I was a broker with Kidder, Peabody. On my first day in the office, I met the guys and was shocked to learn that out of the forty-plus stockbrokers, only three had more than two years' experience. Where had the rest of them gone? Probably to other industries that gave them less intense rejection.

If you want to pick the right candidate during selection, please follow these tips. Number one, call past supervisors. Yes, I know this is a pretty obvious item, but it can yield some of the most important information.

Earlier I mentioned instant replay: the way people bought before is the way they will buy in the future. If you believe this, then you must believe that people don't change. The way they performed on their last job is a very strong indication of what they will do in their next job. Granted, a manager can set the stage for higher success, but success is also predicted by the degree of success the candidate had in his last job.

When I was high school, I bought a Triumph TR4 sports car that caught my seventeen-year-old fancy. The car had very few years on it, but a lot of miles. It was only $400. It sure was the right price. Before I bought it, I took it to a mechanic to be checked out. The mechanic said, "You know, you're going to need a whole new engine overhaul within six months with this thing."

I was shocked. How could he be that specific? I thought, "Nah, he has to be wrong," and I bought the car anyway. I ignored his advice, thinking that I would keep it for a year or two and then sell it before I had a problem. Five months and fifteen days later, guess what? The engine blew up. I spent more money getting it repaired than I had paid for the car.

If you fail to accept the recommendation and analysis of a past employer, you have basically bought yourself a lemon that will cost you more money to fix than it would to buy.

The most important interviewing technique in hiring new telephone salespeople is never, never interview your candidate face-to-face. The biggest mistake that employers make is seeing the person face-to-face and getting so charmed with that person's interpersonal skills that they lose sight of what that person is like on the phone. Don't talk to the person face-to-face except when you offer them a job. You are not trying to find someone who uses great nonverbal techniques, who smiles and has a twinkle in their eye. You're trying to find someone who possesses all those skills, yet communicates them over the telephone.

Here's a tip. Try to interview that person at least three times and spend ten minutes minimum on the telephone every time you talk. You'll find out the level of comfort they have, what their voice sounds like, and how well they conduct themselves. You will also find out how they close the interview. If you like what you hear on the telephone, chances are their prospects are going to like them also.

Number three, make sure you ask your candidate very tough questions. You want that person to divulge as much information over the telephone as possible while being careful not to harass or insult. (By the way, remember to stay within the equal-opportunity laws.) You want to find out what they're happy about. You need to determine what stresses them, what their weaknesses are.

Ask questions like this: "Why do you think you would be successful with my firm?" and "What do you think your biggest strengths and weaknesses are on the phone?" While these have no right or wrong answers, they allow you to see how quickly candidates think on their feet. You might also ask, "What do you dislike the most in a job, and what do you like the best?" Then ask, "What did you dislike about your past employer, and what did you like the best?"

If you can, bear down a little and even voice the type of objections a prospect might give. Some items to keep track of during your telephone interview is whether the candidate can match your vocal patterns. What are the inflections in their voice? Are they pleasant? Does the candidate match your words, or better, use them on you?

Also, does that candidate violate the fifteen-second rule? Do they keep talking after fifteen seconds on the phone? You probably already know that it's much more difficult to teach people skills on the telephone than it is to teach product skills.

If people bought products solely on product information and details, we could all sell online, avoiding a salesperson's contact. We wouldn't have to pay salespeople. But the people skills involved in your business influence about 95 percent of your profitability. Only 5 percent of sales entail product knowledge. People skills help keep those technical skills tailored and focused to help sell your product or service.

You might even say to the candidate, "Things are difficult here. We have a tough time in this business. What would you do to help us increase our sales?" Again, does that candidate pace the objections? How well do they answer the objections you give? Or do they just fold and say, "I don't know if I'm that good"?

When you talk to a candidate on the telephone, you will learn great things. Always realize that the way a candidate acts on the phone with you is how they will act on a prospect call as well. When interviewing on the telephone, you'll learn how they approach and present, and even how they overcome objections, as well as how they close.

Here's another tip. Ask your candidate to call you back for a second telephone interview. Write down the time that you requested the callback. Then write down when they actually do call you back. Did they call at the right time, or did they wait a couple of hours? Did they give you excuses?

They will treat the prospect exactly the way they treated you. It's very easy to teach product knowledge. It's difficult to teach people skills on the phone.

Some time ago, I hired a telephone salesperson. I spoke to the candidate four or five times on the telephone only because my schedule and hers prevented us from a face-to-face meeting. She interviewed extremely well on the telephone. It was a good thing that I didn't see her. She was not the best-looking woman in the world. She was overweight, but she had a super disposition. Her great attitude transferred to her prospects. She was one of the best telephone salespeople I'd had in a long time. I regularly got comments from both prospects and existing clients about how charismatic and enjoyable she was to talk to.

Don't be influenced by a face-to-face interview. Evaluate only how they sound when you are considering their effectiveness on the telephone.

After seven years of training my own staff and teaching salespeople from other companies on how to use the telephone, I've learned that some people enjoy talking to others on the phone as much as making money. I've learned that the contact they have and the enjoyment they receive sometimes makes up for low income. But I have also learned that the first couple of months is an extremely frustrating experience. This is a sharp contrast to the complete enjoyment that they receive when they feel comfortable on the telephone.

If your new telephone rep has a high desire to become better and improve, they'll have a wonderful career ahead of them. If they don't, they'll quit after just a couple of months out of frustration and rejection. You will lose whatever time and money you have invested in them.

How to Develop Great People

Request any new salesperson you hire to read this book at least three times from start to finish. It will help your new employee become more comfortable on the telephone with even the most negative of prospects. More importantly, it will help the novice learn what to expect when embarking on this type of career.

One important point in training salespeople, especially when they're new, is to keep them from overlearning the product details. Your new salesperson has a high built-in desire to learn your product inside and out. This is usually a mistake. I worked with a company a few years ago that had a three-month product-training process before their people were allowed to interact on the telephone. Granted, the products were computer peripherals, which were a little bit more sophisticated than pencils, but a three-month training period was a bit long even for that type of sale. When the new employees eventually did get on the phone, we recorded their interactions. Most of them spent a majority of telephone time telling the prospect how great the product was.

You want the salesperson to let the prospect know that the product is the best in the industry, but the salespeople we evaluated acted like engineers. They gave so much information about the throughput speeds and circuitry of the peripherals that they bored their prospects into comas. The result was they rarely booked appointments, which was their objective in the first place.

In each case, we found that these new trainees would present the product without probing first. They got objection after objection, which they didn't know how to handle. In effect, they rarely got the chance to close.

At the same time, we found that those salespeople who were trained in phone skills and in how to deal effectively with people learned the products more quickly and were able to apply the knowledge much more effectively.

Here's a simple rule in training phone salespeople: Get them to start selling within two weeks after you hire. Help them become familiar with the product, but don't let them overlearn. Help them get an idea of the kind of questions a prospect may ask. Force them, at least initially, to depend on their people skills in order to probe and determine when to present the right product benefits at the right time. They also need to learn to ask the right question at the right moment. Obviously, you don't want to put your new trainees into a position where they're on a level of an Amway salesperson trying to sell Hewlett-Packard test instruments. However, it would be equally disastrous to get an astrophysicist on the phone to sell chiropractic appointments.

Hook that salesperson up to a recorder during a training conversation. Record their real-life conversations for the first three months. Yes, they will be embarrassed. They will probably be stressed as well, but letting them hear what they say on the telephone is like letting a speaker watch himself on video. They will rapidly learn what to say and how they sound. They will also be highly motivated to upgrade their teleselling skills.

Sit with the trainee and listen together to an audio of phone conversations. Ask these very simple questions: "How do you think this could have been improved?" "What did you hear?"

Many managers, when they're training, say, "No, you shouldn't have done it like that. Here's what I would like you to say instead." Frequently trainers lecture rather than facilitating the learning process. Ask the trainee how things could have been improved initially. Give them a chance to build their own skills. They may say, "Oh, yes. I remember you saying this a couple of weeks ago. I should have said what you told me to say then. I'll do that from now on."

As a rule, *never offer more negatives in training than positives*. Generally, offer three times as many positive compliments as constructive criticisms. If you enhance the positives over the negatives, you'll build the employee's self-esteem. As I mentioned previously, during the first few months new producers might quit from the intense rejection. But if you keep trying to build their self-esteem, you will help them achieve a confidence level so that they will overcome the rejection they get on the phone.

Number two, let your trainees tell you how they could have improved before you criticize them.

Number three, ask yourself this question before you begin any training sequence: "What are my goals with this prospect on the phone?" Help each trainee establish clear-cut goals for each call. Help them achieve their goals by offering steps to take that will lead to their outcome.

I once heard a manager say to a phone trainee, "No, you shouldn't have said that to that guy, 'I'd like to book an appointment on Tuesday at 3:00 or Friday at 5:00.' You didn't probe effectively. You had no rapport."

This diatribe went on for at least twenty minutes until the trainee eventually said, "Well, my prospect told me that I had ninety seconds to give him information about my product. When the ninety seconds were up, I tried to close him." For this salesperson, the goal was to present quickly and close quickly. For the manager, the goal was approach and probe. You can see the disparity. They each had different goals.

Next, plan to use the recorder every day for at least three months. After that, record twice a week. Then eventually once a week for the balance of the year. This will be most effective in helping new salespeople develop into superstars.

I insist that anybody who works on my staff record themselves for the first three months. I truly believe that they grow more quickly than do salespeople who have been trained without being recorded. It's one thing to tell trainees what to do. It's another thing when they hear it for themselves.

In addition, allow your phone salespeople, at least for the first few months, to see customers face-to-face as often as possible. Encourage them to take prospects out to lunch or visit their offices. There's a great temptation to stay on the telephone, insulated from seeing that person eyeball to eyeball. This way you help your trainees experience their prospects and clients not just as numbers but as real people. The face-to-face encounters will add incentive. It will let them see whom they're talking to and will more highly motivate them to do a better job.

Lastly, make sure that you set production goals for at least the first year. Prepare a list of their daily, weekly, and monthly dial and contact goals during the first year. Include the people you want them to contact.

One major reason the attrition rate is so high with phone salespeople is that they were never told what was expected, and they never knew specifically how to do it. A manager for a New York Life agency once told me he says, "I'm going to guarantee your success" every new insurance agent that walks into the office. Wow! Then he says, "If you make ten new prospecting phone calls every day and go on two appointments every day, you will close three pieces of business per week. Then you will make the Million Dollar Round Table. If you only do that, you will be totally successful."

That's what your salespeople want from you. They want to know exactly what they have to do to be successful. They don't want to leave anything to chance. They want to be able to gain control of their own production. They want to learn and succeed using you as their trainer, manager, and developer.

Predicting Success

Would you like to know how effective you or your people are at making phone calls? Would you like to be able to predict your success in the future by what you've done in the past? One way to determine this and figure out how much work you're putting into making a sale is to keep records.

Even if you're working hard and making lots of calls, you still may not know what it takes to make a sale. You need to know your averages. How many calls are you making? If you're a face-to-face salesperson, how many telephone calls do you have to make in order to get an appointment? How many appointments do you make to get a close? How many closes does it take to make a sale?

When you have this kind of information at your fingertips, you can see that when calls decrease, closes decrease. When closes decrease, lack of sales will naturally follow.

Sometimes, when calls increase, sales could still decrease. This could mean that motivation is very high, but your effectiveness and your use of techniques for making the phone call are very low. Something is wrong.

Keep records of each of these things. Keep track of how many calls you make. Keep track of what is said during each phone call, whether that person was in, whether they were away from their desk, and whether they will call back. Keep a log on all calls you make during the day. Not only can you look at the number of phone calls you or your salespeople make, but you will also be able to review the conversation. This is a fairly obvious for being a good phone salesperson. But often salespeople keep track of who they call by making notes on the margins of directories, or they just jot a short note and the person's name.

I recommend that you keep all these records using a good customer-relations management (CRM) software. It will enable you to review the names of the people who were scheduled to call back. A good recordkeeping system will also help you keep easy access to callbacks. Review voice mails daily so that you don't rack your mind trying to remember who they are when they call you back.

I remember my first year of teleselling. I didn't have a secretary. I would typically answer the telephone by saying, "This is Kerry Johnson. May I help you?" (All the mistakes, right away.) They would say, "My name is John Thompson. I'm returning your phone call."

I'd made so many calls that I couldn't remember who John Thompson was. Once in a while, I would even have to say, "Gee, I'm sorry. I don't remember you. Can I find your file and call you right back?"

Boy, was this embarrassing! If I had reviewed the previous day's will-call-back file, I would have had John Thompson on the top of my head and the tip of my tongue. Better yet, if I had a good CRM back in those days and reviewed whom I left messages for, it would have saved a lot of embarrassment.

Even if you have an assistant who screens your calls, it's effective if you can review whom you left messages for. But the most important part of recordkeeping for phone calls is to give you a good method of seeing what skills you need to develop. Where should you focus your training? Where should you put your investment dollars? Keeping records is a great way of analyzing results.

Another great way is to keep a chart or graph. One company telemarketing restaurant services actually kept a grease-board wall log and graph of the number of phone calls made each day. They would then graph sales production. They would keep a moving line across the graph as well for everyone to see. The startling fact was that phone calls and sales were loosely related before they started keeping these graphs, but after they did, phone calls went up, and sales in response went up dramatically.

The people who looked at the graph realized their past performance and tried to increase future performance, making more sales. The graph gave them tangible evidence of the effort they put in and the sales that were produced as a result.

How to Compensate Phone-Sales Reps

If you're leading phone salespeople, you have probably wrestled at least once with the question of how to pay them. How much money should you give them to be motivated? What else should you do to maintain that motivation?

There are three ways to pay phone salespeople: (1) by straight commission, (2) by commission plus base salary, and (3) by base salary alone.

Base salary is an effective way to start new people. Often those without phone experience or those who are unfamiliar with a product need a few months of experience to become productive. Because of this, they are often frightened they may not make enough money to live on while they're learning.

Most companies deal with this in a very effective way. Insurance companies offer financing plans of about $1500 to $2000 a month. Brokerage firms frequently do the same. This works well for new people, but not as well for more experienced people.

A commission plus base is an intermediate step to wean telephone producers off a base salary. Often with the commission-base split, you lower the base and increase the commission, depending on how effective that person is.

One technique is to offer telemarketers high commissions or percentages to force them off guaranteed base salary. Sometimes managers pay salespeople a commission plus a base because they're responsible for more than just making phone calls. The base may be compensation for leading a team of other marketers.

In my business, my phone salesperson receives a base salary plus a commission. She often has to send letters and deal with existing clients. She also has to prepare the materials for my appearance at a seminar or conference. This is usually a nonmarketing, nonselling type of activity. If she were solely engaged in selling, this compensation structure would be inappropriate.

Lastly, on the commission-only system, you will find the highest reward for performance. It's like gambling: people tend to put more money into a slot machine and pull the arm more quickly when there is a random reward than they would if there were a predictable, routine reward.

Telephone salespeople in particular always want to make more money and will be increasingly productive as long as they think the commission dollars may come on the next phone call. You will get markedly higher performance out of them if you give them commission only or commission plus base instead of base salary alone.

The best telephone salespeople you have will make more on commission only. Most salespeople that realize any company will never pay them what they're worth on a base salary alone, but they can make as much as they want on a commission. Managers who pay their experienced telephone salespeople on a base plus commission or base salary alone are missing the boat. Top telephone salespeople will double their production overnight if you put greater rewards in their compensation.

Selling or booking appointments on the phone is too difficult without adequate compensation. The rejection is so intense that the salesperson will slack off unless their financial future is linked to actively making calls. They need to know that activity will result in a high income. Obviously, a commission makes for more excited salespeople. They work not only for the satisfaction of knowing they did a good job, but also because they realize their income is linked to their activity. My marketing director will often ring a bell when booking a speech in the office. Sometimes I think this has nearly equal importance to receiving a paycheck.

Would you like to help your phone salespeople become less dependent on you? The answer is to gradually decrease their base salary as you increase their commission. The best salespeople I've had always made more money with a straight commission than salary only.

Years ago, I consulted with one company executive who paid his salespeople on activity. He wanted his producers to make 100 calls a day. He would pay each producer $10 per call. The agreement was that the money was only for a conversation with a prospect. No messages were allowed. They also had to do a presentation to that prospect. This manager very astutely realized that if he could increase activity, he could increase sales. If he could increase the number of people the salespeople talk to, he could increase his overall production.

Often salespeople are not motivated by $10 per phone call or by any amount of money. Sometimes a salesperson is rewarded by other things besides money. These rewards could be a sauna, tennis, or golf—the nonfinancial stuff of life.

You probably also realized that short of giving your sales producers $10 each time they talk to a prospect, you certainly can also give them other types of recognition, such as plaques. You can also create a competition in your office for the greatest activity—perhaps a daily dinner for the greatest number of prospects contacted.

When I was a consultant with a major company years ago, there was an effort created for those new people who were not as experienced as the top producers. Their reward was also based on activity. These awards were usually given out once per month. But in the beginning, once a week. The more frequent the reward, the more impact it has on performance.

Another technique you can use to keep your salespeople's activity high is visual feedback. When you put a graph in front of your telemarketer and ask them to keep a moving activity line of exactly how many calls they make, calls increase.

Whether you base your salesperson's income on straight commission, commission plus salary, or straight salary, matching motivational rewards with money will help to increase their production.

Managing salespeople is much more complex than making calls yourself. You must be a trainer, coach, and counselor, as well as an expert on phone sales. You have to be a cut above every producer you manage. You have to be able to diagnose your producers' problems. You also have to present solutions. You have to provide enough incentive and motivation to keep them calling even in the face of incessant rejection.

These techniques will help you manage, motivate, and lead your phone salespeople more effectively. Try each of these techniques, depending on your goals. I'm sure your management effectiveness and their performance will skyrocket.

Summary

What You Learned in This Book

In this book, you have learned many things about phone sales. Initially, you learned why you need to become effective on the telephone. You need to do more than sell. Phone sales is a specialized set of skills that few people possess. From the first chapter, you learned key concepts about how to approach prospects and existing clients. You learned how to get through assistants and how to get receptionists to help you. You also gained information on getting referrals and what to say to them. One of the nice things about prospecting and selling on the phone is that you are able to communicate with a lot more people than you ever could face-to-face.

Unfortunately, often this includes playing telephone tag. You picked up techniques on getting the prospect or client to call you back sooner. You gained information on how to avoid getting blown off the telephone in the first thirty seconds. You also learned how to use lists.

You learned how to use a script. You learned how not to sound canned. You found out how to use your voice effectively as well as how to listen with power.

Do you remember learning how to increase your level of sincerity and urgency in prospecting? You found out not only how to do this, but how to probe more effectively.

You discovered that the key ingredient to selling on the phone is probing. If you can find out what that prospect wants and needs and then provide solutions, your closing rate will be more than 90 percent.

You discovered key ideas on how to listen for and repeat back your prospect's own words during the probing phase. You learned how to determine how your prospect's mind is organized. You also found out how to reach the decision maker and the steps by which they make decisions. Once you know their decision strategy, you can present the way they want to buy.

You learned how to draw your prospect in by using techniques like the takeaway. Your skills now include how to ask key questions. These include open and closed-end questions as well as how to prepare your prospect for the second call. You learned how to make them more receptive for the second contact as well.

You learned how to connect with an uninterested prospect. You learned how reconfirm needs before presenting product or service solutions.

Do you remember the twelve turnoff phrases? Avoiding these will help you keep the prospect positive.

You learned that stories sell and facts tell. You gained a new skill set in how to tell stories as you explain benefits. You also were given ideas on how to reference-sell.

Do you remember how to trial-close? This is the process to prepare the prospect for the close, helping ensure a 100 percent closing rate.

By now, you are an expert at answering a prospect's objections. You gained six steps to cashing objections in addition to the quick *feel-felt-found* technique.

You also learned how to answer objections like, "I'm not interested," and, "I don't buy from people on the telephone," which you'll often get during the first thirty to sixty seconds on the telephone.

More importantly, you learned how to close. You learned the two most important closes as well as the recommend technique. You also know now how to sell the way your prospect wants to buy instead of how you want to sell.

You gained information on how to transfer urgency in order to help prospects buy more quickly. You learned how to handle difficult customers and clients, as well as how for every customer who complains, there are many others who will never discuss the same issues with you. You learned how complaining customers can become the best repeat clients.

Do you remember how to cross-sell and get add-ons to orders? Add-on selling or upselling other products will help you increase overall production with the same number of customers.

Lastly, you learned how to hire, pay, and motivate qualified phone salespeople. This information on interviewing and sourcing, as well as coaching and counseling, will not only help you to get the right people, but also to develop their skills.

Obviously, I believe that there is a great demand for skills such as the ones you've read about; otherwise I would not have put a book like this together. Sales managers, producers, and professionals who have reviewed this book unanimously agree it will help them double sales. I hope you find the same thing to be true. If I had found a high-content book like this, I would have become much more successful much more quickly when I was starting out in my own business.

In this online age, effective telephone skills are even more important to increasing your business. All major sales begin with online research and end with a phone call.

Every day, you pick up a tool which now you are trained to use.

You are like a lumberjack cutting wood in a forest. He and another lumberjack labored for much of the day cutting down timber, but the first one quit early, having cut substantially more wood than the second, who worked throughout the day.

The second man said to the first, "You know, it seemed like I worked twice as hard as you. You took breaks every hour, a long lunch, and you quit early. How did you cut more wood than me? How did you make more money than me when I worked twice as hard?"

The first lumberjack said, "What you did not realize is that during every break and lunch period, I also sharpened my ax."

This book sharpened your ax. Please read it at least five times from beginning to end to fully incorporate these concepts. I believe that you will increase your production substantially. It will give what you say on the telephone so much impact that your business will skyrocket.

Please also send me a note. Let me know what you liked and disliked. Even more importantly, let me know how you've been able to use these techniques. Can you apply these skills? Have you already used them? I would love to hear from you. You can contact me at

Kerry@KerryJohnson.com
714-368-3650
Twitter: @DrKerryJohnson
Linked In: Kerry Johnson, MBA, PhD
Facebook: Kerry Johnson, MBA, PhD

CPSIA information can be obtained
at www.ICGtesting.com
Printed in the USA
LVHW030227130819
627393LV00006B/8/P